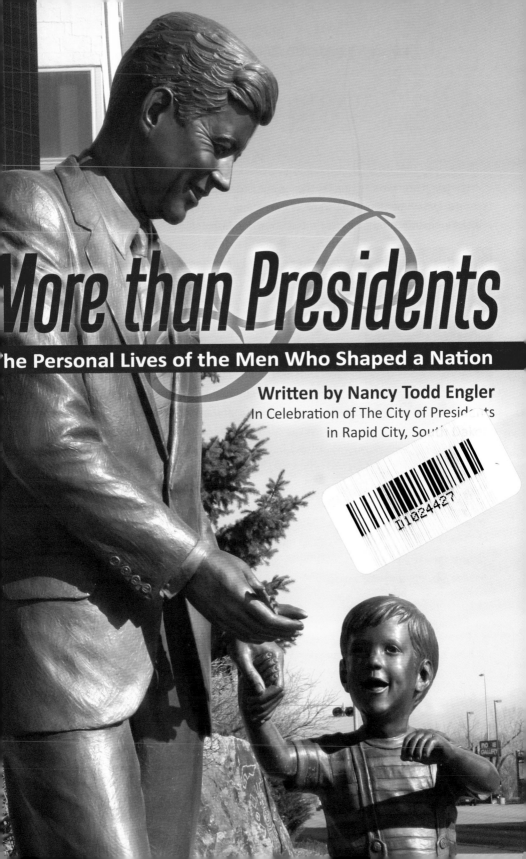

More than Presidents

The Personal Lives of the Men Who Shaped a Nation

Written by Nancy Todd Engler

In Celebration of The City of Presidents
in Rapid City, South Dakota

Published by Simple Solutions 2 Publishing Group
Written by Nancy Todd Engler | www.morethanpresidents.com
Editing & Design by Debbie M. Ketel of Bright Angel Publishing
Printed in the U.S.A.

ISBN: 978-0-615-55292-7

The City of Presidents is a project that demonstrates the ability of a small, committed core of individuals to create something of historic importance and economical impact in the private sector. The City of Presidents is now accessible to people and the media throughout the world.

Rapid City, SD, is the only place in the world where all 42 U. S. presidents can be seen in life-sized bronze statues.

Acknowledgements:

To Debbie Ketel, for patiently guiding me through the scattered thoughts in my head and converting them to beautifully written words.

To John Lopez, The City of Presidents artist, good friend and supporter, for generously providing the photographs for the book.

To Johnny Sundby, for brilliantly supplementing the photographs to enrich the chapters of the book.

To Joan Perdue, the author's biggest cheerleader for many years.

To my daughters (Teri, Susie and Lyn and their families), my sisters (Agnes and Sharon) and especially my husband, Joe, who put his world on hold to allow me to fulfill my dream.

—Nancy Todd Engler

Foreword

In 2000, Don Perdue invited me to serve on the Board of Directors of The City of Presidents and to write short presidential biographies to be on display in the Presidents' Information Center. I was honored to be a part of this monumental (pardon the pun) project. Having been in the hospitality industry of the Black Hills for many years, I knew what an impact such an undertaking would make on Downtown Rapid City.

Soon, the walls of the Presidents' Information Center were lined with short presidential biographies, but it had been difficult and distressing for me to have to edit down the entire personal life of a president of the United States to a single page.

Many visitors began asking for a book that contained all of the presidential biographies. I saw my opportunity to retrieve much of the edited copy from the original stories and expand all of the information into a single book containing more complete biographical stories. Because The City of Presidents is apolitical, I decided to write about the personal lives of the men who would shape this nation instead.

Using more than 20 reference books, I found that specifics varied from book to book. No incident was written in this book unless I could confirm the stories in the majority of my research material. I found history, especially political history, was always open to personal interpretation. My goal was to be impartial, informative and factual. I hope those who read this book will accept it as historical storytelling.

My research found common threads in the lives of these men—the strong influence of family, hard work, religion, service and self-reliance. Many historical stories parallel those in the headlines today.

It is my hope that you will enjoy learning about the nation's leaders on a personal basis and feel that you now know them as people, not just as presidents.

To Jordan,
Thank you for your part in
making my book a success . . . and
always remember to follow your
dream!
Nancy Todd Engle

Contents

**This book is dedicated to the man
who followed his dream . . .
. . . to Don Perdue**

When businessman Don Perdue relocated his company to Rapid City, he noticed the interest around the life-size *Seated Lincoln* sculpture outside the Hotel Alex Johnson. This statue was sculpted by Mount Rushmore artist Gutzun Borglum. He saw how the public interacted with President Lincoln, often having photos taken while sitting next to him. Perdue recognized this as an asset to the Rapid City economy and thought: "What if

The City of Presidents' Don Perdue

statues stood on every street corner of the downtown area?" After seeing Mount Rushmore, a visitor could see the rest of the men who shaped American history. *The dream began.*

In February 1999 during a Rapid City Lincoln Day dinner, Perdue shared his ideas with Dallerie Davis, a Black Hills realtor and active member of the artist community. Dallerie was sure she knew artists who would commit of this project. The original artists were John Lopez, Lee Leuning and Sherri Treeby, James Michael Maher and Ed Hlavka. James Van Nuys was later included in the team. (See artists' biographies, p. 5).

The artists did extensive research into the lives of each president. They and the board of directors agreed that they did not want to create static portraits of men in suits standing on the street corners. Each statue was to give some insight into the personality and the presidency of its subject. *The dream was becoming a reality.*

The cost for all 42 presidents would be $2 million dollars—all to be raised through private donations and not government funding. The intention was to place the statues on the corners of Rapid City's downtown, giving an identity to the city as well as having an artistic and economical impact. Slowly, the benefactors came forward and The City of Presidents was born. *The dream was almost complete.*

In 2000, the first four U. S. presidents were placed on the street corners of Rapid City. In 2002, Perdue purchased an historic building in the downtown area and established the Presidents' Information Center, which was designed to resemble the White House's Oval Office. Visitors now can view maquettes (miniature versions of the statues) and can read presidential biographies displayed on the walls.

In October 2010, the final four statues were placed, and the project was completed. On the day of the final unveilings, members of the Central High School Class of 1956 were honored for their continuing maintenance of the statues. Perdue also invited local Boy Scout troops to attend the ceremony so he could thank them for their years of tending to the appearance of the statues.

After hearing the story of Mr. Perdue's dream, the scouts were asked to stand and give their gift to him by reciting, "I will follow my dream—because I can make a difference!"

The Artists

EDWARD E. HLAVKA

One of the country's most prolific sculptors, Hlavka's work includes figurative bronzes depicting wildlife, western, southwestern, jazz, children, religious and ethnic themes. Born in Sturgis, SD, Edward developed an interest in sculpture at a young age. His unique ability to portray characterizations delight the many people across the country who view and collect his art. Exactness of detail, whimsy and grace of figurative design are hallmarks of Hlavka's work.

JOHN LOPEZ

Sculptor John Lopez grew up on a ranch in South Dakota. His life has always held an aura of creative energy. A college sculpting class led him to a career in art, beginning with classical Western wildlife and rodeo-themed bronzes. Early in his career, he was invited to be one of The City of Presidents' sculptors, sculpting 12 presidents. John now divides his time between bronze and hybrid metal art. Working from a background of vast anatomical knowledge, he welds together scrap iron and weaves in bronze castings in hide-and-seek fashion. A special hybrid occurs under the torch of John's creative fire.

JAMES MICHAEL MAHER

Jim notes, "As an artist, I begin from a belief that the human form is the elemental ground of art, and that line, form and gesture have the power to engage and strike a cord that resonates within. I seek forms that transcend mere physical likeness and give insight to the true nature of my subject, and the nature common to all. I draw strength from the Black Hills, which has always seemed to me to be a very sculptural place, both in its heritage of artists and its essential forms." Spiritual art is a dominant theme for Jim.

LEE LEUNING AND SHERRI TREEBY

Lee Leuning and Sherri Treeby have placed over 70 life-sized sculptures nationwide. Selected in 1999 by The City of Presidents' Foundation, they have sculpted 11 of the 43 presidents. In 2001, they were selected from a large field of artists to create this nation's first state World War II monument in Pierre, SD. They also created the state's Vietnam and Korean War memorials. Lee and Sherri incorporate high realism and a sense of Americana in all their works.

JAMES VAN NUYS

Realistic painter and sculptor James Van Nuys was born in Whittier, CA, in 1955 and has lived intermittently in Rapid City for most of his life. He attended Wilmington College in Ohio, graduating with a double major in art and music. Returning to the Black Hills in 1982, be began to apply his formidable rendering skills to the landscape that he loves—the Black Hills, the Badlands and the small, forgotten prairie towns that dot the map of western South Dakota. His work can be seen in his gallery at 516 Sixth Street in downtown Rapid City.

Photo Credits

Photos by John Lopez:
Front Cover, Back Cover pp. 36, 40, 44, 48, 52, 56, 60, 68, 72, 76, 80, 84, 88, 92, 100, 104, 112, 116, 120, 124, 128, 132, 136, 148, 156, 164, 168

Photos by Johnny Sundby Photography:
pp. 3, 8, 12, 16, 18, 20, 24, 28, 32, 64, 68, 70, 78, 96, 108, 110, 130, 134, 138, 140, 142, 144, 146, 152, 160, 172

The artists' photos were supplied by each artist.

All other presidential photos are considered public domain by wikipedia and have been attributed to the author when known.

George Washington

In Washington's time, it was very common for biographers to write stories about notable people to emphasize their personal traits. One of the stories written about Washington was the account of young George chopping down a cherry tree, which was not true. Although Washington never chopped down a cherry tree, the story was perpetuated as a tribute to Washington's integrity and honesty, even as a child.

Portrait by Gilbert Stuart

The other story frequently told about George concerned his wooden teeth. In fact, he had very painful problems with his teeth throughout his entire life. Most pictures show him with his mouth closed, as his false teeth were also very painful. Although wooden teeth were tried (along with ivory, gold and lead), he wore dentures carved from hippopotamus teeth most of the time.

His physical appearance was striking. He was extremely tall, standing well over six feet with reddish hair and blue eyes. Stricken with smallpox as a young adult, George's face was badly scarred. Portrait painter Gilbert Stuart, after studying the president's face, remarked that "it was the face of a man with tremendous passion subdued by an iron will." His carriage was graceful, and he was known to write love poems in his notebooks.

George was born on the family estate near Pope's Creek in Westmoreland County, VA, to Augustine Washington and Mary Ball Washington on February 22, 1732. George came from a large family of three older stepbrothers, three younger brothers and a sister. The Washington family was Episcopalian, but, instead of following a formal religion, George fashioned a moral code of right and wrong for himself and rigidly adhered to his own standards.

George expected to follow in his brothers' footsteps and go to school in England, but those dreams were shattered when he was 11 years old and his father died. Instead, young George attended a local school taught by ministers and was mainly self-taught after the age

Artist Concept:

Washington is portrayed as a general in full military dress attire. Before he was known as a politician, he was known as a military commander. At 6' 2", he was also a tall man for his time. Depicted in a prideful military stature, he is shown at possibly his finest hour.

Sculptor: Lee Leuning | Benefactor: Great Western Bank and Trust

of 14. He was an average student in most studies but excelled in mathematics. The lack of a good education was to be one of the great sorrows of his life.

At the age of 13, George found his grandfather's surveying tools and, with his love of numbers and mathematics, learned to survey land. At the age of 17, he became the official surveyor of Culpepper County, VA, and was given the generous wage of $7.20 per day.

George spent a great deal of time with his stepbrother, Lawrence, who owned Mount Vernon, because he wanted to escape from his complaining, domineering and overprotective mother. His mother constantly complained to her son, even during his presidency, about needing more money and attention although she was very well provided for. Because of her constant nagging, she was never invited to George's home later in life.

During his frequent visits to Mount Vernon, George learned the finer skills and polished manners of a gentleman such as horsemanship, dancing, fencing, card playing and social graces. George looked upon Lawrence as a substitute father. However, when George was 19 years old, Lawrence contracted tuberculosis. Although George took him all the way to the West Indies for a cure, Lawrence died and George came down with smallpox, which almost killed him.

At the age of 21, George inherited his father's 260-acre family farm near Fredericksburg, VA. He also received half of a 4000-acre tract of land, 10 slaves and a portion of his father's personal wealth. In 1752, George also inherited Mount Vernon from Lawrence's estate. The estate included 2,500 acres and 18 slaves. Although George did own slaves, he treated them with care. George's will ordered all slaves on his land to be freed upon his death.

At the age of 29, Washington sought a wife to help him with the farm. He had developed strong feelings for 18-year-old Sally Fairfax, but she was married to his close friend and neighbor. George then met 27-year-old widow Martha Dandridge Custis, mother of two children. She was the richest widow in Virginia, inheriting 6000 acres of land and 100 slaves. While engaged to Martha, Washington wrote a note declaring his love to Sally. Although the relationship probably never got beyond the flirtation stage, George and Sally had very strong feelings for each other. Heartbroken as he was, Washington grew to love Martha, and they were a very happy couple.

George and Martha were married on January 6, 1759. The couple was unable to have children so George adopted Martha's children, John Park Custis (Jackie) and Martha Parke Custis (Patsy). He became a devoted and loving father to the children.

In September 1774, the First Continental Congress gathered to discuss their concerns of British rule and taxation. Washington represented Virginia. The radical Patrick Henry was asked who the most impressive member of the Congress was. He replied, "If you speak of solid information and sound judgment, Colonel Washington is unquestionably the greatest man on the floor."

After the Battle of Lexington and Concord began on April 18, 1775, Washington attended the Second Continental Congress in Philadelphia. Dressed in his full military uniform, Washington sent a silent message that he was ready for war, if necessary. John

Adams realized someone must lead the militiamen readying for this inevitable war. There was a unanimous vote calling for Washington to become the commander in chief of the Continental Army. He was 43 years old.

Washington was inaugurated as the first president of the United States in New York City on April 30, 1789, at the age of 57. During his inaugural speech to Congress, he seemed shaken with emotion. "This great man," described Senator William Maclay, "was agitated more than ever he was by the leveled cannon or pointed musket. He trembled and several times could scarce make out to read." At his inauguration, President Washington decided against the regalia of military or royal clothing. He chose to wear a simple brown suit. The tradition of the president-elect wearing American-made clothes during the inauguration is still carried on to this day.

In March 1797, at the age of 65, he finally returned to Mount Vernon after serving eight years as president. Washington worked with architects to design the building we now know as the White House in Washington, D. C. Just before his 68th birthday, on December 12, 1799, Washington went out for his customary ride through Mount Vernon. He became chilled and damp from the snowy day, and he died on December 14, 1799, while taking his own pulse. At the time of his death, George Washington was one of the richest men in America with holdings of 33,000 acres of land, $25,000 in stocks, 640 sheep, 329 cows, 42 mules and 20 workhorses.

Washington's greatness was in his courage and humility. It was said that he gained power by giving it up. He is not remembered for being a great general or battlefield tactician but as a great military leader and administrator who learned from his mistakes. President Washington was once quoted as saying, "I hope I shall possess firmness and virtue enough to maintain what I consider the most enviable of all titles, the character of an honest man."

George Washington left behind no children of his own. Instead he left a nation that he served as its first commander in chief and as its president. He was "first in war, first in peace and first in the hearts of his countrymen." That is why he is rightfully known as "The Father of His Country."

Mount Vernon.

Second President of the United States of America

John Adams

President John Adams was described by Benjamin Franklin as ". . . a man who means well for his country, is always an honest man, often a wise man, but sometimes, and in some things, absolutely out of his senses." In fact, John Adams was a brilliant man but, at the same time, insecure and stubborn. Those of his time described him as scholarly, rude, urbane, irascible, jealous, paranoid, suspicious and more.

Portrait by Asher Durand

Born on October 30, 1735, in Braintree, MA, John was named after his father who was a politician, militiaman and farmer. John Adams was a short, stocky man (5'6" tall) who lived to the age of 90 despite a life of poor health exacerbated by a smoking habit that began at the age of eight years old.

As a child, John was lax in his schoolwork due to the lack of supervision and favored hunting instead. He was known to bring a gun to school so he could start hunting on his way home.

John cared little for school, but he was found to have a gifted intellect. At the age of ten, his father asked him, "What would you do, child?" and John answered, "Be a farmer." His father took John to the fields and worked him as hard as any adult, returning home in the evening tired, sore and covered in dirt. His father asked again, "Well, John, are you satisfied with being a farmer?" He hoped his son had learned a valuable lesson. Instead, John answered "I like it very well, sir." The Adams men were obviously very stubborn.

John was taught to read by his father, and his favorite subject was mathematics. Although he had little patience for schooling, he agreed to be more attentive if his father allowed him to study with Joseph Marsh, a man who ran a more challenging school. John's schoolwork improved, and he entered Harvard at the age of 16. He originally studied to become a schoolmaster, although his interests were more toward the law. He felt that teaching allowed little to stimulate him intellectually and soon became bored as a schoolmaster. To escape this humdrum life, Adams settled on practicing law.

When John Adams, Sr., passed away in 1761, John gained his father's place in the

Artist Concept:

Adams was a great orator. After Thomas Jefferson wrote the Declaration of Independence, Adams presented it to Congress "with a power of thought and expression that moved us from our seats." Adams is shown delivering an oratory dressed in the formal dress of his time period.

Sculptor: John Lopez | Benefactor: Stanford Adelstein

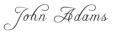

Braintree Town Meeting. This began his political career. As British rule continued to weigh heavy costs on the colonies, he became more and more passionate about independence from England.

In 1764, John Adams married Abigail Smith. They moved from Braintree to Boston to further John's law career. Although Abigail had absolutely no formal education, she became John's closest friend and wisest political advisor. Some historians say that Abigail was the true power behind the presidency and was the first feminist in American history. She once wrote to her husband to "remember the ladies" when making laws for the new nation. "Do not put unlimited powers in the hands of husbands," she said.

Adams's high profile in the law resulted in him being elected to the Massachusetts legislature in 1770. A few months later, both John and Abigail were troubled by ill health. They made the decision to leave political life and return to Braintree where Adams could resume his law practice and farming. He was quoted as saying, "Let me have my farm, family and goose quill, and all the honors and offices this world has to bestow may go to those who deserve them better and desire them more. I court them not." However, after their health improved, the Adamses returned to Boston.

As a member of the Massachusetts legislature, Adams attended the First and Second Continental Congress. He fought tirelessly and impatiently to establish the colonies' independence.

After Thomas Jefferson wrote the Declaration of Independence, it was John Adams who presented it to Congress. Jefferson said that Adams spoke "with a power of thought and expression that moved us from our seats." After much debate, Congress adopted the Declaration of Independence despite the nervousness of the delegates to take the next step toward independence. Sometimes thought of as being overly self-righteous, Adams assured them that he was prepared to take full responsibility for the consequences of this declaration. His willingness to take the blame for their actions made even the most concerned delegates go along with him.

Adams served in France and Holland in diplomatic roles during the Revolutionary War. During the time he was serving as minister to the Court of St. James, his position was abolished. Finding himself without an official appointment, Adams returned home. Members of the Electoral College voted John Adams as vice president under George Washington. While serving as vice president, Adams felt frustrated. He complained to Abigail, "My country has in its wisdom contrived for me the most insignificant office that ever the invention of man contrived or his imagination conceived. "

President Washington served two terms in office and declined to consider a third term. A general election was held to choose a new president. At that time in history, the candidate with the highest number of votes became president. The second highest number became vice president. As a result, Thomas Jefferson, a Republican, became vice president under President John Adams, a Federalist. Thus, the two most important political positions in the new country represented two different political parties.

John Adams

John Adams was inaugurated as the second president of the United States on March 4, 1797. John, Abigail and their four children became the first presidential family to live in the White House.

During his presidential term, Adams was confronted with a number of issues, including the threat of war with France. He attempted to make a strong stand against France without going to war. This set Thomas Jefferson against Adams, as Jefferson had always been friendly toward the French.

The presidential nominations of 1800 increased the tension between Adams and Jefferson. When the votes were counted, Vice-President Thomas Jefferson won. The outgoing president was stunned and felt rejected by the country he had served so long and so passionately. On the day of Jefferson's inauguration, Adams left alone, too hurt to attend.

Adams spent his last 25 years on his farm in Braintree. One of his greatest joys was that he lived to see his son, John Quincy, sworn in as the sixth president of the United States in 1824.

Twelve years after he left the White House, Adams and Jefferson resumed their friendship that continued for the remainder of their lives. Some believe that a heartfelt letter of condolence from Abigail Adams to Jefferson after the death of his wife led to a softening of resentments.

On July 4, 1826, 50 years to the day after signing the Declaration of Independence, near noon, Adams woke from a deep sleep and spoke his last words, "Thomas Jefferson survives." He died later that day. Unknown to Adams, Jefferson had died at 12:50 p.m. earlier the same day.

Historically, Adams ranks as one of the greatest American political philosophers.

Painting by John Trumbull

John Adams and others present the Declaration of Independence to Congress.

Thomas Jefferson

Thomas Jefferson changed the world, and he did it with a pen. He was the first secretary of state, the second vice president and the third president of the United States.

Born on April 13, 1743, in the Blue Ridge Mountains of Virginia, Thomas was born to Colonel Peter and Jane Jefferson. His mother was from a wealthy British family of high social standing. His father kept a close eye on Thomas's education and taught him to read and write at a very early age. The elder Jefferson had a library of more than 200 books, including the works of Shakespeare, and young Thomas had read all of them by the age of six.

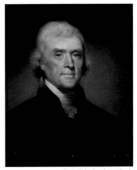

Portrait by Rembrant Peale

Thomas's father excelled in mathematics, and Thomas learned it all quickly. He learned to survey land, draw maps and keep accounts. He became a proficient hunter, strong swimmer and an excellent rider. When Thomas was just nine years old, he was studying Greek, Latin and French.

At the age of 14, Thomas's father died very suddenly. Peter left the plantation to Thomas and his brother and left his books, writing desk and surveying tools to Thomas. This inheritance helped him become an expert mathematician who could design buildings, perform medical operations like an experienced surgeon and play the violin. Called "Long Thomas" by his friends, he was a six-foot-tall, very thin redheaded man with broad shoulders.

At the age of 17, Thomas enrolled in the College of William and Mary in Williamsburg, VA. There he studied calculus, physics, natural science, agriculture, astronomy, chemistry, history and languages. He began writing on every thought and observation he had in notebooks. For the rest of his life, he chronicled the minute details of his surroundings, including the price of an egg and the planting of crops.

After finishing college in 1762, Jefferson decided to study law. In 1764, he turned 21 and assumed responsibility for his family, his slaves and the work on the plantation. Thomas began his law practice in 1767. Although he had never formally studied architecture, he

Artist Concept:

Jefferson is depicted writing the Declaration of Independence. From up close, the entire document can be seen on this statue. Jefferson appears to be looking away from his work—as if looking to the future.

Sculptor: Ed Hlavka | Benefactors: Dr. Ed and Peg Seljeskog

designed and supervised the building of his Monticello home.

In December 1768, 25-year-old Thomas Jefferson entered politics when he was elected to the Virginia House of Burgesses. While in Williamsburg, Thomas met Martha Wayles Skelton, a 20-year-old widow with a three-year-old son who died a few years later. On January 1, 1772, Thomas and Martha married and then had a daughter, Martha, in

Of Note: **Jefferson's hand on the Declaration.**

September of 1772. Mrs. Jefferson's father died shortly after she was married, and she inherited 11,000 acres of land, 135 slaves, 669 books and a large debt. The Jefferson's then had a second daughter, Jane, who died shortly after she was born.

Although not able to attend the First Continental Congress, Jefferson did represent Virginia at the Second Continental Congress. There, Congress chose five men to write America's Declaration of Independence—Thomas Jefferson, John Adams, Benjamin Franklin, Roger Sherman and Robert Livingston. Adams said that Jefferson was the man to do the writing. Thomas retired to his room for 17 days and wrote and rewrote until he thought every word was perfect. In his original draft of the Declaration of Independence, he proposed the abolition of slavery but was later overruled due to the fear that the southern colonies would reject this and refuse to ratify this declaration.

Adams and Franklin thought the declaration was elegant and made very few changes. The document was then presented to the entire Congress on June 28, 1776, and was met with great debate. Finally, on the evening of July 4, 1776, the delegates walked to the desk and signed their names to the Declaration of Independence. In keeping with his obsessive note-taking, Jefferson recorded the temperatures at varying times of day on each day. The temperature of the room at the time of the signing was 73.5 degrees Fahrenheit.

The next few years were life changing for the Jeffersons. In May of 1777, Martha presented Thomas with his first-born son, but the baby died one month later. The following August, her fourth child, Polly, was born. In June 1779, Jefferson was elected governor of Virginia. In April of 1780, a fifth child was born. Unfortunately, shortly after the birth, this child also died. At the end of his term as governor, a weary Jefferson retired to his beloved Monticello.

The spring of 1782 found a happy, contented Jefferson. Martha gave birth to their sixth child, Lucy, born strong and healthy. However, after the birth, Martha became weaker and weaker, and she died on September 6, 1782, with her husband at her bedside. In his desperate need to regain control of his life, Jefferson went to work on his library. He listed every one of his 2640 books, made a list of each of his 240 slaves and constructed a list of every letter he had ever written.

Jefferson was then elected as the Virginia delegate to Congress. In May 1784, Jefferson was asked to go to France to work with Adams and Franklin on trade agreements. There, he received the dreadful news from Virginia that his two-year-old daughter, Lucy, had died.

While in France, Thomas heard his friend, James Madison, was helping write the Constitution. Jefferson wrote of his concerns that there was nothing being included about the rights of people. He wrote, "Human rights were at least as important as property rights."

George Washington was elected as the new country's first president, and Jefferson's name was proposed as the first secretary of state. Jefferson accepted the invitation and, in February 1790, took the post.

Soon the Democrat-Republicans convinced Jefferson to run against Adams for the presidency. The election was very close, but Adams received the most electoral votes and became the second president. The law at that time dictated that the man who came in second became vice president. On March 4, 1797, President John Adams and Vice-President Thomas Jefferson were sworn into office.

During his first term as president, Adams and Jefferson were often in disagreement, and Adams rarely spoke to Jefferson. Two years into his vice presidency, Jefferson returned to his home and stayed there most of the year. It was at that time that Jefferson decided to run against Adams for the next presidential election. When it was over, Jefferson was elected the third president of the United States and took the oath of office on March 4, 1801. He chose Madison to be secretary of state. It wasn't until years later that Jefferson and Adams renewed their friendship. Some believe that a heartfelt letter of condolence from Abigail Adams to Jefferson after the death of his wife led to a softening of resentments.

Jefferson realized the importance of incorporating the Mississippi River for the new nation's trade agreements. He bought the entire Louisiana Territory of almost a million square miles for $15 million dollars (or three cents an acre) from French Emperor Napoleon Bonaparte. As a result, President Jefferson doubled the size of our country. In May 1804, Jefferson commissioned Meriwether Lewis and William Clark to explore this new frontier. He could not see them off on their journey, as he had to return to Monticello to be with his married daughter, Polly, while she was in childbirth, but she died before he arrived. Of the six children born to Thomas and Martha, only one daughter, Martha, outlived him.

Jefferson ran for the presidency again in 1804 and won by a landslide. However, this term as president had its challenges. His decision to declare a trade embargo against England backfired, and his former vice president, Aaron Burr, staged a smear campaign against Jefferson. This led to Jefferson's desire to leave political life and return to Monticello. As he began his retirement, Jefferson found himself deeply in debt. He paid off his father-in-law's debts, which put Jefferson further in debt. By 1826, Jefferson owed over $100,000.

In 1826, at the age of 83, Thomas Jefferson became very ill. On July 3, he knew he was dying but fought to live one more day. Jefferson then died on July 4, 1826, which was the 50th anniversary of the signing of the Declaration of Independence. Just a few hours later, his friend, John Adams, died on the very same day.

Thomas Jefferson created a vision for a new country. Much of the foundation upon which our nation is built came from the mind and the pen of this one man.

Fourth President of the United States of America

James Madison

Thomas Jefferson once said of his long-time friend, James Madison, that "he was the greatest man in the world." Although he was only 5' 4" tall and weighed just 100 pounds, Madison was an intellectual giant, giving him the name, "the great little Madison."

James Madison, Jr., was born on March 16, 1751, in the fertile Piedmont section of Orange County, VA. The Madison family owned Montpelier, which was a plantation of 5,000 acres of land and at least 100 slaves. James was the first-born son of 14 children born to James and Nelly Madison. Although James was a sickly child with epileptic-like symptoms, what he lacked in physical strength was compensated by his extraordinary intelligence.

White House Historical Association

At the age of 11, a schoolmaster from Edinburg University educated James. This tutor recognized James's academic strength and introduced him to mathematics, science, Latin, Greek and French. Later in life, Madison stated, "All I have been in my life I owe largely to that man." Thanks to his tutor, Madison entered Princeton University, and his excellent education allowed him to complete his college studies in two years. However, the strain left him so weak and ill that he returned home to Montpelier when his epilepsy-like attacks returned.

When war broke out against the British in 1775, Madison was commissioned as colonel in the Orange County militia. However, his frail health limited his activities to conducting drills, target practice and recruiting. In 1776, he served on the Virginia House of Delegates to adopt a new constitution for Virginia.

In 1784, Madison was again elected to the Virginia House of Delegates and attended the First Constitutional Convention in 1787 in Philadelphia. Despite his weak and insignificant appearance, Madison's arguments were strong. Madison earned the title, "Father of the Constitution," for his role in drafting much of the document. After many days of writing and re-writing the Constitution, all the delegates present signed the document in September 1787.

Artist Concept:

Madison was small in stature and did not have a strong speaking voice. Since he wasn't a great orator, he chose to be behind the scenes. He is depicted with his finger at a page in a reference book.

Sculptor: Lee Leuning | Benefactors: Bill and Pete Duhamel

In January 1789, George Washington was elected as the first president of the United States. In February 1789, Madison was elected to the House of Representatives. Washington recognized Madison's knowledge and skill in the use of language and asked Madison's advice about Washington's inaugural address. Madison wrote the final speech that Washington delivered.

When the debate arose regarding the permanent location of the Capitol, Madison won over the vote to permanently place the Capitol in Washington instead of New York or Philadelphia. Of all his accomplishments in helping to set the country on a steady course, Madison's work on the Bill of Rights was his greatest achievement. Madison fought the hardest for the freedom of religion, an issue of separation of church and state that is still being challenged today.

In 1794, Madison met and married Dolley Payne Todd, a beautiful 26-six-year-old widow with a three-year-old son. Although there was a 17-year difference in their ages, Dolley and James enjoyed a very happy marriage. Dolley became famous for her popularity and talent for entertaining. She held her own place in history for the role she played in the political scene.

By the end of Washington's second term, Madison had become frustrated and disillusioned with the divisions that had begun between the Federalists and the Democratic-Republican parties. Madison decided to return to his home at Montpelier and resume his role as a Virginia planter.

When Jefferson became president in 1800, he called on Madison to serve as secretary of state. He agreed to take this post to serve his friend and political ally. Madison supported President Jefferson's Louisiana Purchase that doubled the size of this new emerging country. After his second term as president, Jefferson encouraged Madison to run for the presidency to assure that their party's belief in democracy and individual rights would continue.

James Madison became the fourth president in 1808 after defeating James Monroe. Madison soon became aware that he had inherited many of the problems of the Jefferson presidency, especially in foreign affairs. The real problems of trade agreements with England and France were growing to the point that war seemed inevitable. Madison tried everything to settle these issues peacefully, but he eventually signed the official declaration of war on June 18, 1812. It was later said that there were three things that sustained Madison during these trying times—Dolley, his strong intellectual powers and his belief in the United States of America.

Madison was re-elected in November 1812. England was on American soil, and his troops were poorly trained. In August 1814, British troops marched on Washington. Dolley escaped with her husband's papers, some treasured books and a portrait of Washington. The British soldiers proceeded to burn down the president's house and all that was in it. They went on to burn many government buildings, including the Capitol. The war waged on, and the British press called for President Madison's resignation. The British attacked on all quarters—north and south—and it wasn't until Andrew Jackson's Battle of New Orleans in January 1815 that a peace treaty was signed by the British. The new peace opened trade again, manufacturing increased and housing boomed. The entire world recognized this new American nation, and respect for the United States was not questioned.

Madison chose not to run for a third term and supported his friend, James Monroe, for the presidency. John Adams was quoted as saying that Madison's administration "notwithstanding a thousand faults and blunders, has acquired more glory and established more union than all his three predecessors."

In the spring of 1817, the Madisons returned to Montpelier. There, Madison and Jefferson became even closer friends, sharing common interests in agriculture and expansion of educational opportunities such as public schools, universities and the military academy at West Point. Madison's health declined in his last years, and he died on June 28, 1836, and was buried at his beloved Montpelier at the age of 85. After his death, Dolley returned to Washington and then died on July 12, 1849.

Madison was probably the best-educated president to serve this country. His service to his new country spanned 60 years. Former Treasury-Secretary Albert Gallatin in 1817 praised Madison stating, "Never has a country left in a more flourishing situation than the United States at the end of your administration; and they are more united at home and respected abroad than at any period since the war of the independence."

Painting by Michel Corne

The USS Constitution during the War of 1812.

James Monroe

As a very small child, James Monroe remembered listening to conversations between his father and George Washington in his parents' home. General Washington's stories of the wilderness and the wars he fought enthralled James.

The future president of the United States was born on April 28, 1758, in Westmoreland, VA, in a family of three brothers and one sister. James was an active boy with a love of riding, hunting and farming. He was known to attend school with his books in one hand and his gun in the other. Living in a home of modest income, James brought home wild game to add meat to his family's table.

At the age of 11, James attended the local Campbelltown Academy where he studied the classics, mathematics and Latin. He also learned the ideals of loyalty, honesty, honor and devotion.

White House Historical Association

When James's father, Spencer, died, his estate allowed James to travel to Williamsburg, VA, to attend the College of William and Mary. His earlier education prepared him well in Latin and mathematics, and the college accelerated him to an upper-level class. About the same time James was in college, the politics of the colonies heated up. The students of William and Mary were caught up in the excitement and joined the town's militia. In 1776, at the age of 17, James left school to join the Third Virginia Regiment. A few months later, James's regiment was called to fight the British, and they joined George Washington's army in the north. His regiment held off nearly 1,500 British until reinforcements arrived. During the battles, Lieutenant Monroe was seriously wounded. After recuperating from his wounds, he was promoted to captain and then joined his men at Valley Forge. There, he made friendships with people from Europe, widening his knowledge of the world. One of his friends was Marquis de Lafayette. The new friend introduced him to Greek and Roman philosophy, emphasizing civic duty and social responsibility. This influenced him for the rest of his political life.

Artist Concept:

Monroe was known to be a very cordial man—someone of charming demeanor who always carried a cane. He is shown tipping his top hat, wishing passersby a "good day." He is believed to have begun the politician's custom of kissing babies to charm constituents.

Sculptor: Lee Leuning | Benefactor: Walt Hall Family

During the war, Monroe, the militiaman, met Thomas Jefferson, the politician. A friendship began that lasted for nearly 50 years. In fact, it was Jefferson who advised Monroe to study law.

In 1783, Monroe began his political life with the help of General Washington and his friend, Jefferson. Monroe won a seat in the Virginia House of Delegates. By 1785, Monroe was becoming a power in Congress, chairing many of the most important committees.

While participating in the New York social scene, 27-year-old Monroe met 17-year-old Elizabeth Forthright. Elizabeth was a tall beauty with the education and social graces to be a perfect political hostess. James and Elizabeth were married on February 16, 1786. In December of that year, their first daughter, Eliza, was born.

When his term in Congress expired, Monroe decided to retire from politics and return to the practice of law. In 1788, he served at the Virginia Ratifying Convention where he voted against Virginia's ratification of the Constitution until he was assured that the Bill of Rights would be adopted.

In 1790, 32-year-old Monroe was elected as one of the two senators from Virginia. During Monroe's senatorial term, the general public was not allowed to observe Senate debates. Monroe fought for and won a motion to change this rule. To this day, the public has the right to sit in the balcony and watch Congress at work.

In 1794, President Washington appointed Monroe as minister to France. He recognized that Monroe's friendship with Marquis de Lafayette would hold him in good stead with the French government. It was Washington's desire for Monroe to maintain a neutral stand with France while the United States pursued a treaty with Great Britain. When the French learned of America's alliance with Great Britain, the country broke off their relationship with America. President Washington blamed Monroe for failing to convince the French to accept the treaty, and Monroe was recalled to America.

Monroe left the political scene in 1798, which proved to be a very dark year for him. He returned to farming and practicing law. Unfortunately, both farming and the law did not bring in enough money to support his family, and he fell deeper in debt.

In 1799, the people of Virginia again called Monroe back to politics, electing him governor of Virginia. That year, he also celebrated the birth of a son, James Spence Monroe. The following year, his son was stricken with smallpox and died. In 1802, Elizabeth gave birth to their second daughter, Maria Hester.

During Monroe's third year as governor, President Jefferson requested that James return to France as special ambassador. France owned land in the middle of the country called Louisiana, and Jefferson wanted to purchase New Orleans to assure permanent access to the Mississippi River. Monroe was authorized by Congress to buy this land for up to $10 million dollars. However, Emperor Napoleon Bonaparte wanted to sell the whole territory of Louisiana. Ambassador Monroe and American Minister Robert R. Livingstone knew that time was of the essence and struck a deal with France for $15 million dollars, purchasing all of Louisiana. President Jefferson brought the treaty before Congress and after much debate, it was approved. The United States of America became larger in size than most of the major powers in Europe.

Monroe's next few years found him back in politics, serving under Jefferson's successor, James Madison, as secretary of state. At the outbreak of the War of 1812, President Madison's secretary of war resigned, and Monroe served in the dual role of secretary of state and secretary of war until the war ended in 1815. Monroe was seen as the man responsible for the conclusion of the war with Britain, and his path to the presidency was in place.

In the national election of 1816, Monroe became the fifth president of the United States. President Monroe was elected to a second term, and he sent his seventh annual message to Congress in December 1823. His address included a statement that "American continents . . . are henceforth not to be considered as subjects for future colonization by any European powers." He had just formulated an important American policy that later became the Monroe Doctrine.

Monroe's secretary of state, John Quincy Adams, succeeded Monroe as sixth president of the United States in 1824. Monroe took no interest in the election, as his wife, Elizabeth, had become seriously ill and his indebtedness grew worse. By the time he had retired from public office, he owed $7,500 (or the equivalent of over $1 million dollars today). Monroe even resorted to presenting a bill to Congress for his expenses during his ambassadorship and presidency. Congress finally awarded him less than half of what he requested.

On September 23, 1830, James's beloved Elizabeth died. He found he could no longer live at Oak Hill without her, so he sold his home and moved to New York City. He began suffering from a nagging cough (possibly tuberculosis) and died peacefully on July 4, 1831. Monroe was the third of the first five presidents to die on the Fourth of July.

Monroe was an example of the best type of public servant. In his lifetime, he served as a soldier, diplomat, governor, U.S. senator, secretary of state, secretary of war and president. Monroe's friend and mentor, Thomas Jefferson, described him this way: "Monroe was so honest that if you turned his soul inside out there would not be a spot on it."

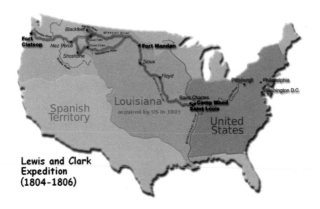

Lewis and Clark
Expedition
(1804-1806)

John Quincy Adams

One of John Quincy Adams's most vivid childhood memories was that of standing with his mother, Abigail, watching the Battle of Bunker Hill from atop Penn's Hill. He later said this event marked a conscious dedication to the cause of freedom that he carried with him the rest of his life.

White House Historical Association
Portrait by George Healy

The son of the second president of the United States was raised in the throes of the American Revolution. Johnny was born John Quincy Adams on July 11, 1767, the first-born son of President John Adams and Abigail Smith Adams. His mother was a devoted and active patriot, often sending Johnny to town to gather information about British soldiers' activities that she passed on in her many letters to her husband. On one occasion, Johnny walked into his house and found his mother melting her spoons to make bullets. Years later while recalling this incident, Adams wrote, "Do you wonder that a boy of seven who witnessed this scene should be a patriot?"

John Quincy's birthplace was Braintree, MA. Two years before Johnny was born, his mother gave birth to a daughter named Abigail (Nabby). A daughter, Suki, was born in 1768, but died two years later. Abigail then gave birth to two more sons—Charles and Thomas Boylston.

Although John's father was absent from home a great deal of the time, the elder John believed strongly in the importance of education for his sons. He instructed Abigail in the studies he felt were important, although Johnny preferred his own type of reading such as fairy tales and adventure stories. During the war, Abigail became a teacher to her sons, instilling morality to their studies, duty to family and society, religion, virtue, hard work and the love of learning in her children.

When Congress sent John Adams to France as a commissioner, 10-year-old Johnny begged his father to let him go along. Abigail gave her blessing, believing that he could spend more time with his often-absentee father and pursue an education in Europe. John

Artist Concept:

Adams was not a casual man in any sense of the word and was always dressed in full formal dress with top hat and cane. Here he is portrayed as the man he was on all occasions.

Sculptor: John Lopez | Benefactors: First Western Bank and Patrick Roseland

Adams tempered his strict rules of schooling for his son by introducing him to the society of Europe. As a teenager, he stood beside his father at the signing of the Treaty of Paris, which formalized America's independence.

At the age of 14 while in Paris, John became smitten by a young actress about his same age. He never worked up the courage to visit her backstage, but he continued to be enamored with her for over two years. "Of all the ungratified longings that I ever suffered," he admitted, "that of being acquainted with her, merely to tell her how much I adored her, that was the most intense."

Like his father, John Quincy returned to America to attend Harvard University when he was a young man. He was a very serious and competitive student, graduating as an honor student in only two years and rated as second in his 1787 Harvard class.

John Quincy kept a daily diary, not missing a single day. Adams once wrote, "There has perhaps not been another individual of the human race whose daily existence from early childhood to fourscore years has been noted down with his own hand so minutely as mine."

Adams chose to practice law. John became a practicing lawyer and was driven to compare himself to his father, wanting to exceed his accomplishments. By 1790, he had passed the bar and was an established lawyer in Boston with an interest in politics.

In 1794, at the age of 27, Adams gave up his law practice for the life of a foreign diplomat. While serving in London, John met Louisa Catherine Johnson, who was the British-born daughter of an American counsel. On July 26, 1797, John and Louisa were married in London. Louise Catherine was the only foreign-born first lady in U. S. history. John Adams originally had objections to his son's marriage because he did not think it wise for a future president to have a foreign wife. Abigail did not receive the news well either.

In 1800, John was called back to America, and Louisa gave birth to their first son, George Washington Adams, just before their return to America.

After resuming his political career in America, John Quincy was elected to the U. S. Senate in February 1803. That same year, Louisa gave birth to their second son, John Adams II, who was named after his grandfather.

While serving as a U.S. senator, Adams allied himself with President Thomas Jefferson on the Embargo Act, which prohibited trade ships from traveling between Britain and the United States. Unfortunately, the act backfired, and Adams was unseated in his post in Congress. It was during this time that the Adams's third son, Charles Francis Adams, was born.

With his pride severely damaged, Adams resumed his law practice and believed that his political career was at an end. However, in 1809, President James Madison appointed Adams to a diplomatic assignment in Russia. While there, he developed a strong personal friendship with Czar Alexander I, so much so that the czar became godfather to their infant daughter, Louisa Catherine, who died tragically before her first birthday.

Adams was then summoned back to America in 1817. President James Monroe had appointed him secretary of state. His efforts in this position resulted in making America a

strong, independent world power through the Monroe Doctrine. Bolstered by his success in the cabinet, he dared to dream about the presidency.

Adams declared his candidacy for the 1824 presidency, but he knew that General Andrew Jackson was also becoming very popular in the political ring. In order to offset Jackson from entering the presidential race, Adams asked him to be his vice-presidential running mate. However, Jackson chose to enter the primary race against Adams instead.

In the primary election, Jackson heavily defeated Adams by the popular vote. However, in the presidential election, states' votes gave the presidency to Adams, and John Quincy took the oath of office at the age of 57 on March 4, 1825.

In his first message to Congress, Adams spoke of the creation of the Department of the Interior, a reform of existing patent laws, the development of a national university and military academy, and the financing of scientific exploration. Due to his unpopular political views and a vigorous, dirty campaign against him, Adams was defeated by General Jackson in the 1828 presidential election. Adams was so upset over the loss that he chose not to attend the inauguration. Like his father, he unceremoniously left the Capitol and returned to his home.

Believing his public life was over, John and Louisa planned to retire to their family home in Massachusetts, but fate had not finished with John Quincy Adams yet. When the congressional seat in Adams's district was vacated, friends encouraged him to run for it. John Quincy believed that he still had something to offer the country, and the challenge was irresistible. In 1830, at the age of 63, Adams was easily elected to the 22nd Congress and became the only former president to serve as a U. S. representative.

One of John Quincy's lasting legacies was the construction of the Smithsonian Institution because he convinced fellow congressmen to accept a gift bequeathed to the U. S. by British chemist James Smithson to establish a building that honored the knowledge of man.

Adams continued to serve in Congress, despite his failing health. On February 21, 1848, after casting a vote in the House of Representatives, he collapsed in his chair from a massive stroke and died two days later. Senator Thomas Hart Benton said, "Where could death have found him but at the post of duty?"

Historians write differing opinions of John Quincy Adams's presidency. He was a man of great accomplishments diplomatically and of modest presidential success. It was a life lived fully, right to the day of his death.

Seventh President of the United States of America

Andrew Jackson

Andrew Jackson was a new breed of presidential stock. The men before him were educated aristocrats and authors of the American Revolution. On the other hand, Jackson was a firebrand, a duelist, an Indian fighter and a man who had fought the wars of his country since the age of 13. Although one of the most popular presidents of the common man, he was one of the most poorly educated. He could not spell or compose a proper sentence, but he could speak powerfully and eloquently about the things of which he felt passionate.

Jackson was notorious for his volatile character. His hot temper, prickly sense of honor and sensitivity to insult often embroiled him in fights and brawls. In 1806, a minor misunderstanding over a horse race ended in a duel with pistols between Jackson and Charles Dickinson. Dickinson, a crack shot, fired first and hit Jackson square in the chest. Jackson gave no sign of being hurt but coolly stood his ground, aimed carefully and killed the man. Jackson carried that bullet for the rest of his life. Later, in 1813, Jackson fought in a Nashville, TN, street brawl where he took a bullet that nearly cost him an arm.

Temper aside, it could be said that Jackson fulfilled the American dream. Born and raised in the back country of South Carolina to poor Scotch-Irish immigrants, young Andrew was very much a part of the colonies' rebellion against British rule. His father, Andrew, Sr., died the day before young Andrew was born on March 15, 1767. His mother, Elizabeth, became the widowed mother of three children. The Jackson's had to move into the home of his aunt, the Crawford's, where Elizabeth cared for the eight Crawford children as well as her own three sons.

The Jackson boys grew up on their mother's chilling stories of how the Irish mistreated their grandfather under British rule. Her hatred of those who destroyed the rights of others was instilled into her sons. Andrew's older brother, Hugh, was the first to go to war and died of heat and fatigue in 1779 at the Battle of Stone Ferry.

Artist Concept:

Jackson is depicted as a man of defiance—a characteristic that dominated his life. With military uniform billowing and arms sternly folded, the true attitude of the man is shown.

Sculptor: James Michael Maher | Benefactors: Arthur and Sarah Ludwick

One year later, Andrew, and his brother, Robert, joined the mounted militia. In 1781, after a skirmish with the British, the Jackson brothers were captured. When ordered to shine a British officer's boots, Andrew refused and was struck by the officer's sword, which cut Jackson's left hand to the bone and badly injured his face and head. The resulting scars remained for the rest of Jackson's life.

Mrs. Jackson heard of her sons' imprisonment and went to the prison to plead for their release. Both boys were very weak from lack of food and infections from battle scars. In addition, they were burning up with fever from smallpox. Elizabeth was able to gain the boys' release and began the grueling 40-mile trip back to their home. Upon their arrival, Robert died, and Andrew was near death. With his mother's loving care, he regained his strength and slowly recovered. His mother then joined other women who went to Charleston to care for prisoners of war. Unfortunately, she became ill with cholera and died a few months later.

After the deaths of his mother and brothers, the now orphaned 15-year-old Andrew wandered from relative to relative. Andrew realized he wanted to do more with his life and returned to school. At the age of 17, young Jackson rode to Salisbury, NC, to study law. After studying for two years in a law office in Salisbury, Andrew moved into the office of one of the most brilliant lawyers in North Carolina—Colonel John Stokes. He did what was expected of him but little more. In his spare time, he gambled, drank, chased women and took dancing lessons. Regardless of his extracurricular activities, he appeared before two judges who authorized Jackson to practice law in North Carolina on September 16, 1787.

In 1791, Jackson entered a liaison with Rachel Donelson Robards, the daughter of John Donelson, who was one of Nashville's founders. Rachel was married but separated from her husband, Lewis Robards of Kentucky. Some stories say that Rachel believed that Robards had filed for divorce, and she was free to remarry. Rachel and Andrew began living as man and wife and didn't marry formally until 1794 when Robards procured a divorce. These circumstances came back to haunt Jackson in his presidential campaigns, when opponents charged him with bigamy and wife-stealing. However, Andrew and Rachel's marriage was a perfect match. They were deeply devoted to each other and remained so until Rachel's death in 1828, just after Jackson was elected president. Jackson was devastated and entered the White House as a bereaved widower who never got over his wife's death.

Jackson's formal military career began in 1812 when he was made major general of the Tennessee militia. During the War of 1812, he earned a reputation as an Indian fighter by defeating the Creeks in a number of important battles. Serving under Jackson in these battles was a 21-year-old ensign named Sam Houston. Jackson once said of Houston, "A man made by God and not by a tailor."

Soon after his victory at the Battle of New Orleans in 1815, his name surfaced as a possible presidential candidate. Jackson felt differently though. "I know what I am fit for," he said. "I can command a body of men in a rough way, but I am not fit to be a president."

By 1824, he reconsidered his decision, and he won more popular votes and electoral votes than the other three candidates in the first popular presidential election. However, he did not win an outright majority of electoral votes as constitutionally required. As a result, the choice fell to the House of Representatives, and they chose John Quincy Adams. Adams had waged a smear campaign against Jackson, citing evidence of adultery against Jackson for having lived with Rachel before her divorce was final.

In 1828, Jackson supporters formed the Democratic Party for the express purpose of electing Jackson for president, and he won an easy victory in 1828. He went on to serve a second term, describing his presidency as, "I can with truth say mine is a situation of dignified slavery."

Jackson retired from office on March 4, 1837, at the age of 70. Although suffering from tuberculosis and dropsy, his daily routine was busy. He remained an advisor to those seeking public office and continued to stay connected to the common people who loved him and raised him to the highest post in the land. He died quietly on June 8, 1845, at the age of 78 at The Hermitage, the home where he and Rachel had spent so many happy years.

Jackson's powerful personality played an instrumental role in his presidency. His character polarized contemporaries and continues to divide historians. Some praise his strength and audacity, while others see him as vengeful and self-obsessed. To admirers, he stands as a shining symbol of American accomplishment—the ultimate individualist and democrat. To detractors, he appears an incipient tyrant, the closest we have yet to come to an American Caesar. Part of him remained the frontier hero, Indian fighter and scrapper, but his heroism took him places higher than he ever dreamed.

Painting by Edward Moran

Andrew Jackson at the Battle of New Orleans during the War of 1812.

1837–1841
Eighth President of the United States of America

Martin Van Buren

In his political life, Martin Van Buren was known as the "Little Magician," referring to his reputation as a cunning and wily political broker rather than for his short stature. Van Buren was the first politician to work the political party system, often trading jobs for favors and eliminating positions of those who opposed his views.

Van Buren was the first president born under the flag of the United States of America, entering this world after the Revolutionary War. Born December 5, 1782, in Kinderhook, NY, Martin was the son of Abraham and Marie Hoes Van Buren. His mother had been widowed with three children before she married his father. They went on to have six more children.

White House Historical Association
Portrait by George Healy

According to some sources, it was Van Buren who was the inspiration for the word "O.K." One of his nicknames was "Old Kinderhook" from his childhood birthplace. People showed approval of Van Buren and his policies by using the term "O.K."

Martin's father owned a farmhouse. The first floor was the local tavern and polling place. Abraham was a politically active man, and his tavern became the gathering place for conversations about the emerging nation. Politicians and lawyers met and dined with the Van Burens, and Martin's greatest education came from the conversations he overheard in the tavern. With such a large family, the Van Burens were not wealthy, and, as soon as the children were old enough, they pitched in and worked the family farm.

With so much work to do on the farm, Martin only occasionally attended his local school. As a result, his reading and writing skills were poor, and his lack of education haunted Martin throughout his entire life. During his presidency, he wrote, "How often have I felt the necessity of a regular course of reading to sustain me in my conflicts with abler and better-educated men."

By the age of 14, his school days ended, and Martin left home to apprentice with a lawyer. His jobs consisted of sweeping floors, tending the fireplace, copying legal notes in

Artist Concept:

Van Buren is seated on a bench, eloquently dressed and reading his local newspaper—the Kinderhook. *The sculptor placed him there to allow interaction with the visiting public, creating an opportunity for a photograph with one of the presidents.*

Sculptor: Edward Hlavka | Benefactors: Dr. Edward and Peg Seljeskog

longhand and learning the legal profession. At 15, he presented his first legal argument to a local court.

He stayed with the lawyer's family during his five-year apprenticeship, adopting the manners and tastes of his wealthy surroundings. His family was unable to provide Martin with the clothes needed to enter the professional world, but he soon began wearing the well-tailored outfits of his master. Although less than 5'6" tall, his elegant appearance made him a striking figure in his new social status.

At the age of 21, Martin completed his law studies and was admitted to the bar. In 1803, he returned to Kinderhook and began a successful law practice, building a reputation as a zealous and resourceful lawyer.

On February 21, 1807, Van Buren married his distant cousin named Hannah Hoes. Hanna and Martin had four sons—Abraham, Martin, John and Smith. Unfortunately, after only 12 years of marriage, Hannah died of tuberculosis. Very little is written about Van Buren's family life, and his autobiography contains no mention of Hannah at all. Although Van Buren never remarried, he had a reputation for being flirtatious, especially with married women.

In 1812, at the age of 30, Van Buren's legal successes made it possible for him to run successfully for the New York state senate during the War of 1812. He worked diligently for the success of the American militia's defeat of the British. He introduced a bill in the New York senate to abolish debtor's prisons. In his first term as state senator, Van Buren was also appointed state attorney general.

During this period of history, steamboats were expanding the possibilities of inland commerce. New York recognized the need for a canal that would link the Hudson River with the Great Lakes. Although Van Buren recognized the canal's importance to New York, he did not want to support a project that would need federal funding. As he often did when he took an unpopular stand, he tried to disguise his actions. After originally opposing the project, he had a dramatic change of mind. He worked hard to persuade dissenting senators to vote for the construction of the Erie Canal. The real reason he changed his mind was to garner votes from the New Yorkers who wanted the project. Although this was strictly a decision made for political gain, many people felt that it was Van Buren who saved the Erie Canal for New York.

Because of his stance on the Erie Canal, he was fired as attorney general. As a result, he decided to form his own branch of the Democrat-Republican Party. He used what is now a familiar political method called "patronage," which allows someone in political power to hire or fire whomever they wish and trade jobs for political support.

Van Buren moved politics into a new era. He strongly supported the party system and is known as the father of the Democratic Party. After being elected to the state senate in 1821, the power of his party organization and political cleverness made him a powerful senator. He gained a reputation for landing on the winning side of a controversial issue, often changing his mind at the critical time of public opinion. He quickly built a power base that benefited him throughout his political career.

He was always a strong supporter of Andrew Jackson. They ran on the policies of a minimalist government, marking the beginning of the Democratic Party. Van Buren was elected governor of New York in 1829 but resigned a few weeks later to become secretary of state under President Jackson.

Stories of Van Buren's propensity for evasion and double-talk were legion and gained him another nickname of "The Red Fox of Kinderhook." He delighted in telling stories on himself. His reputation for cunning came to the forefront again when he and Jackson recognized that members of the cabinet were of a political faction not compatible with their own. Van Buren approached all the cabinet to resign (himself included) and allow Jackson to reorganize. Following Van Buren's example, they all submitted their resignations, and Jackson accepted them all! The cabinet was then recreated with Van Buren's party members. The "Little Magician" became Jackson's running mate for his successful re-election in 1832.

During most of his second term as president, Jackson was in failing health, and, with Jackson's blessings, Van Buren ran for president in 1836. There were varying views about Van Buren's ability to run the country. He was called a "crawling reptile" and someone who seemed to care for nothing except power. However, the general population believed that Van Buren stood for the same things that their beloved Andrew Jackson did. He had always fought for the common man while other politicians merely helped the rich get richer. On March 4, 1837, newly elected Martin Van Buren was sworn in as the eighth president of the United States.

As quickly as the celebration of his presidency came, the disaster of the most serious economic crisis in the country's history hit. People lived in the streets with no food. The banks failed because the gold and silver of the economy were sent west to purchase land and bankers were forced to issue paper credits. After much delay, President Van Buren finally introduced a recommendation to establish an independent treasury system to remove the government's funds from all banks and issue $10 million in government bonds to relieve the government's financial embarrassment.

During his campaign for re-election in 1844, Van Buren spoke out strongly against the annexation of Texas to the U. S. Being an anti-slavery proponent, he felt that Texas, as a pro-slavery state, would upset the balance of power in favor of slavery in the country. This created great dissent, and Van Buren lost his party's nomination for president.

Van Buren returned to Kinderhook and enjoyed the life of a retired president. He worked hard for the election of Abraham Lincoln, believing that slavery could no longer exist in America. He was once quoted as saying, "As to the presidency, the two happiest days of my life were those of my entry upon the office and of my surrender of it." He passed away on July 24, 1862, at the age of 79 and was buried in the Van Buren family plot next to his wife, Hannah.

Ninth President of the United States of America

William Harrison

William Henry Harrison established many presidential benchmarks, even though he was president for only one month. He had the distinction of being the last president born under British rule. Despite his birth into a family of wealth and privilege, Harrison adopted the common-man presidential campaign slogan of "Log Cabin and Hard Cider." This became the nation's first modern political campaign and served as a model for future presidential races. In addition, when running for president, Harrison was the first candidate to deliver his own political speeches.

White House Historical Association

Unfortunately, Harrison was also the first president to die while in office and given a state funeral, succumbing to pneumonia only 30 days after his inaugural address. The president had delivered a one-hour and forty-minute speech, refusing to wear a coat or hat on that cold and rainy day, which contributed to his demise. In fact, Harrison's inaugural address remains the longest in American history.

Harrison was born on February 9, 1773, in Charles City County, VA, the youngest of seven children. His father, Colonel Benjamin Harrison, was a close friend of George Washington and one of the original signers of the Declaration of Independence. Harrison's mother, Elizabeth Bassett Harrison, came from a well-respected Virginia family.

When William was seven years old, Brigadier General Benedict Arnold attacked the Harrison plantation, stripping the home of furnishings, slaughtering livestock and taking their slaves. The Harrisons had advance warning of Arnold's arrival, so they escaped personal harm, but the invasion affected young William deeply.

At the age of 14, William entered Hampden-Sydney College and then went on to a medical school in Philadelphia. Upon the death of his father, most of the family's wealth went to the oldest child, so William was left with little money and was forced to leave school. Young Harrison then joined the army, receiving an officer's commission from President Washington himself. Coming from a family of privilege, Ensign Harrison found

Artist Concept:

Sitting on a grand pedestal, Harrison is depicted in all his military splendor with a flowing cape and holding his general's hat. Since he achieved the post of major general during the War of 1812, the sculptor wanted to show the elegance of his high military position and his presidential demeanor.
Sculptor: John Lopez | Benefactors: Action Mechanical, American Electric, Black Hills Molding, Powell Shoe Corp. and US Bank

military life desolate and dangerous.

In August, 1794, three years after he had joined the army, Lieutenant Harrison served as aide-de-camp to Major General Anthony Wayne. Harrison was with Wayne when his troops were heading for the British's Fort Miami. This British fort was supplying guns to the Indians in their fight against the Americans. Harrison was excited as he prepared for his first real battle. Adding to this excitement was the fact that General Wayne was planning to use Harrison's battle plan for the impending skirmish.

Harrison fought valiantly in the thick of the battle and encouraged the men to fight courageously as well. As a result, Harrison was commended for his bravery. One officer explained that "where the hottest of the action raged, there we could see Harrison upon his horse, Fearnaught, giving the order." Another officer stated, "If Harrison continues as a military man, he will be a second Washington."

The following year, General Wayne died, and Harrison was given command of Fort Washington in the Northern Territory. Later that year, while visiting Lexington, KY, he met and fell in love with a beautiful and well-educated Anna Tuthill Symmes. Anna's father, Judge John Symmes, strongly disapproved of a marriage to a lowly soldier. Determined to marry despite the judge's wishes, 21-year-old Harrison and Anna Symmes were wed privately when her father was on a business trip. When Harrison encountered Judge Symmes after the marriage, Symmes asked him how he intended to support his bride. Harrison replied, "By my sword and my own right arm, sir." Harrison and Symmes eventually became close friends.

William and Anna had ten children—four of them living long enough to see their father become president. One of Harrison's grandchildren, Benjamin Harrison, became the 23rd president of the United States in 1889.

In 1798, Harrison left the military and was named secretary of the Northwest Territory by President John Adams. In 1800, Adams appointed Harrison the first governor of the Indian Territory. Part of his duty was to buy as much land as possible for the U. S. government from the Indians. In the Treaty of Fort Wayne in 1809, the U. S. obtained three million acres of land in exchange for only $200 per year to each tribe that signed the treaty. After a failed meeting between Governor Harrison and Chief Tecumseh regarding the treaty, the Indians began raiding American settlements. In 1811, Governor Harrison led 1,000 men in the Battle of Tippecanoe, defeating Tecumseh and his warriors. Harrison's victory enhanced his fame as a great leader and earned him the nickname—"Old Tippecanoe."

After the War of 1812, Harrison left the army and retired to his farm near Cincinnati, OH, a national hero. The war, however, put the Harrisons in deep financial trouble. His annual army pay of $2,400 was not enough to support his wife and ten children. So, he made the decision to enter the political arena, which paid much more. He won a position as U. S. congressman from Ohio in 1816 and went on to the Ohio state senate for two years in 1819.

After returning to his home in 1819, Harrison tried farming again, but he was unable

to sustain his family's financial needs. He won a seat in the U. S. Senate in 1825. In 1828, President Adams appointed Harrison as the first U. S. minister to Columbia. With the lure of a salary of $9,000, 49-year-old Harrison accepted the appointment as much for financial security as political aspirations. However, immediately upon his arrival in Columbia, he received news of being replaced on orders by newly elected President Andrew Jackson.

By 1832, Harrison's life had taken some tragic turns. Upon returning to America, Harrison was in debt for over $20,000, and he assumed the responsibilities for two of his son's families who had financial problems of their own. Floods wiped out their crops, and Harrison became seriously ill for months. As a result, he was forced to take a lowly position as clerk of court. Oddly, the Whig party found the once-wealthy Harrison's misfortunes and lowly circumstances attractive for a candidate running against President Martin Van Buren, who was famous for his elegant dress and manners.

Harrison lost his first run for the presidency in 1836 but ran again in 1840 on a platform of being an honest country man and famous military leader. His campaign slogans were "Tippecanoe and Tyler Too" (John Tyler was Harrison's vice-presidential running mate) and "Log Cabin and Hard Cider." Since there was a severe economic depression under President Van Buren, Harrison ran as a "common man." In truth, Harrison had been a wealthy aristocrat who grew up on a plantation with 22 rooms and many servants. In the end, it didn't matter. The public bought the fabricated image, and Harrison went on to be elected as the ninth president of the United States in 1840.

On January 26, 1841, Harrison spoke to an Ohio crowd as he left for his inauguration in Washington, D.C. He spoke somberly: "Gentlemen and fellow citizens, perhaps this may be the last time I may have the pleasure of speaking to you on earth or seeing you. I . . . bid you farewell."

Sixty-eight-year-old Harrison took the oath of office on a cold, wet and wintry day on March 4, 1841, and died on April 4, 1841. Despite the fact that Harrison was president for a short time, he took his oath of office very seriously and was deeply committed to the nation throughout his life.

John Tyler

"Tippecanoe and Tyler, too!" That was the slogan that was being splashed all over the country as the Whig party campaigned to put William Henry Harrison in the White House. Harrison was the hero of the Battle of Tippecanoe and his running mate, John Tyler, was chosen primarily because he was a southern gentleman who could draw southern votes. At that time in history, the office of the vice president didn't carry much importance in the political scheme of things. Little did the country or Tyler realize just how important his role would be until the new president died of pneumonia just 30 days after the election, and Tyler was thrust into the role of president of the United States.

Portrait by George Healy

Placing little importance on his own vice presidency, Tyler had returned to his home in Virginia after Harrison's inauguration. At 5:00 a.m. on April 5, 1841, Tyler was awakened by a knock on his door. Messengers handed him an official letter notifying him that President Harrison had died, and Tyler immediately left for Washington, D. C.

The Constitution of the United States had not made provision for the succession of the death of a seated president. The cabinet, chosen by Harrison, decided that Tyler should be considered "Vice President, Acting President." Some even referred to him as "His Accidency." His cabinet made it clear to him that his involvement in running the country would be neither required nor tolerated.

John Tyler would have none of this. Tyler recognized that abdicating his power to the cabinet "would amount to a declaration to the world that our system of government had failed." He stated, ". . . I, as president, shall be responsible for my administration." He told the cabinet, "I shall be glad to have you with me. When you think otherwise, your resignation will be accepted." Thus, the new president had no allies in the cabinet or in Congress. Congress even resorted to refusing him funds for the upkeep of the White House, forcing Tyler to pay these costs out of his own limited resources. In January 1843, threats of impeachment broke out, and Tyler and his servants were driven to defend themselves

Artist Concept:

As a young man, Tyler dreamed and studied to become an accomplished concert violinist, but he ended up pursuing the law instead. Upon receiving encouraging letters from Tyler's current family members, the artist chose to depict Tyler with his beloved violin.

Sculptor: Lee Leuning | Benefactors: Antonia and Ethan Hamilton, Frank Simpson family, Wells Fargo and M.D.U

with weapons during a march on the White House. Having broken allegiance with both the Democratic party and the Whigs, he served as a president without a party throughout his four years.

Due to his experience, Tyler declared that, upon the death of a seated president in the future, vice presidents would take the office with the full power of the president . One way that Tyler demanded respect as president was to return all mail addressed to "Acting President" unopened.

It was no surprise that Tyler was a man to be reckoned with. Born on March 29, 1790, John was born to a family of southern politicians, as his father once served as governor of Virginia. His parents, Judge John Tyler and Mary Armistead Tyler, had eight children. Living on the family 1200-acre estate called Greenway Plantation, John had a happy childhood. His father spent hours under a huge willow tree in the front yard, playing his violin and entertaining his children with great stories of the American Revolution.

John was also headstrong, inheriting a fiery spirit from his father. It is said that as a young student, he and other classmates suffered under the hand of a strict schoolmaster who physically abused his students. Under John's leadership, the teacher was thrown down, tied up and locked in a closet. Adults who knew of the schoolmaster's abuses expressed no sympathy for the teacher.

In 1802, John entered William and Mary College at the young age of 12. His academic interests were in ancient history, law and political science, but he envisioned himself a musician and accomplished violinist. After graduation in 1807, Tyler began studying the law with his father. It was destined that law, not music, would be his future.

By the early age of 19, John was admitted to the bar in 1809. One year earlier, John met a beautiful daughter of another wealthy Virginia planter. After a five-year courtship, John and Letitia Christian were married on March 29, 1813. Accounts of Letitia described her as shy, pious and selfless, with a deep devotion to her husband and their seven children. Theirs was a very happy marriage until 1839 when Letitia suffered a paralytic stroke, leaving her a bed-ridden invalid until her death in September, 1842, only 19 months after her husband became president.

Tyler's political career began in 1811 when he was only 21 years old and was elected to the Virginia legislature. A year later, Tyler served briefly in military service near Richmond, VA, during the War of 1812.

Tyler was re-elected to the Virginia House of Delegates for the next five years. At 26, Tyler went to Washington, D. C., to serve in the House of Representatives. Tyler, like his father, supported states' rights and worked diligently to prevent making the federal government more powerful. When at odds with other politicians, he always remained faithful to the wording of the Constitution. He was re-elected in 1816, but the bitter debates between the Northern industrial states and the Southern slave states left Tyler discouraged and ill. He resigned from Congress in 1821 and returned to Virginia.

His retirement was short-lived. Encouraged to run again for the Virginia House of

Delegates, he returned to public office and was elected governor of Virginia in 1825. Two years later, the popular governor was elected to the U. S. Senate, due to his hard work in his home state. He became a member of the newly established Democratic Party, which was against a strong central government.

In 1836, Tyler left the Senate and the Democratic party when Democratic President Andrew Jackson became too powerful. Tyler joined a newly formed Whig party that opposed Jackson. Although the Whigs were defeated in 1840 by Democratic Martin Van Buren, they won the 1844 election with the Whig ticket of William Henry Harrison and John Tyler.

Despite their differences, President Tyler and the Whig Congress enacted some positive legislation after Harrison's death. One such success was the "Log-Cabin" bill, which enabled a settler to claim 160 acres of land (and pay $1.25 an acre for it) before it was offered publicly for sale. His legislation also included the Webster-Ashburton Treaty, which settled boundary disputes with Canada, established the U. S. as a participant in policing African illegal slave trade and pushed through a resolution to annex Texas.

Upon his retirement in March 1845, Tyler and his second wife, Juliet Tyler, returned to their plantation in Virginia nearly bankrupt. Tyler was so poor that he was unable to pay a bill for $1.25 until he had sold his corn crop. Five years after leaving office, he and his wife went on to have seven more children. All told, Tyler had 15 children—the most children any U. S. president has ever had. Tyler's youngest child was born in 1860 when Tyler was 70 years old.

Tyler continued his political involvement during retirement, especially during peace talks to try to keep the nation out of a civil war. Due to Lincoln's stand on slavery, southern states began to secede from the Union, and Tyler could not stand to see his country divided. By serving the Confederate Congress, Tyler essentially gave up his U. S. citizenship until President Jimmy Carter restored his citizenship to the United States in the 1980.

On January 18, 1862, 71-year-old Tyler died, considered a traitor by the Union but a hero by the South.

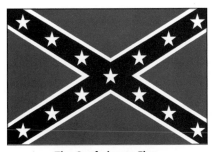

The Confederate Flag.

James Polk

President James Knox Polk was once asked to describe his work habits. He responded, "In truth, though I occupy a very high position, I am the hardest working man in this country." Biographers have reported James Polk as one of the most underrated presidents in America's history. He was a classic overachiever and one of the hardest working presidents, keeping his administration free of corruption and scandal. He also kept every one of his campaign promises, making him quite unique on the list of American presidents.

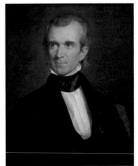

Portrait by George Healy

James was born on November 2, 1795, on the family farm in Mecklenburg County, N.C. James's father, Samuel, and his mother, Jane Knox, married shortly after Jane's father's death. Both Samuel and Jane received a bountiful inheritance, beginning their married life in material comfort. Unfortunately, James, their firstborn of ten children, was a small, frail child prone to childhood diseases.

When James was ten years old, his family moved to the Duck River Valley of Tennessee where the family established a plantation on thousands of acres of inherited land. James, being frail, was unable to work alongside his brothers and sisters. In 1812, he became critically ill. Medical care was lacking, so James and an uncle rode 230 miles on horseback to reach a doctor in Danville, KY. Diagnosed with gallstones, James had to rest several weeks before he was strong enough for surgery. In unsanitary conditions, strapped to a table and given only brandy for the pain, young James survived this risky operation.

Jane Polk taught all her children the strict Presbyterian belief of the "gospel of duty," stressing hard work, never wasting time and accepting their lives without complaint. James embraced these lessons and became a self-contained child. Although his parents had given James only a basic home-taught education, James wanted a proper one. In 1813, 17-year-old James enrolled in Presbyterian Academy where he began his formal education. Within a year, he progressed to a private school in Murfreesboro where he met Sarah Childress, who

Artist Concept:

Polk is shown in the typical dress of the mid-1800s and presented in a political tradition of the times: conducting a cracker-barrel session with local townsmen. The banner on the barrel is the slogan for his 1844 presidential campaign.

Sculptor: Lee Leuning | Benefactors: Arthur and Sara Ludwick

was the 12-year-old sister of a classmate named Anderson Childress. James never realized that one day Sarah would be his wife and the country's first lady.

At the age of 21, James entered the University of North Carolina with grades good enough to put him in the second-year class. He found he had a talent and passion for debate and soon became interested in politics. In 1818, Polk graduated from the university with the highest honors in mathematics and the classics.

After graduation, James went to Nashville to study law with Felix Grundy, who was a famous criminal attorney. James followed his passion for the law and politics and passed the Tennessee bar in 1820. He opened his own law office in Columbia. In 1823, after serving for two years as a state senate clerk as well as continuing in his own law practice, 28-year-old Polk decided to run for elective office.

Because his mother respected Andrew Jackson, James admired him as well. When Polk made the decision to enter public life, he sought the advice of Jackson, who told him, "You must settle down as a sober married man with one who will never give you any trouble. Her wealth, family, education, health and appearance should all be superior. You know such a woman well." Polk knew that Sarah Childress was especially close to Jackson. Polk asked, "You mean Sarah Childress? I shall go at once and ask her." He became so enamored with the sophisticated, educated and beautiful woman that he rode 50 miles on horseback to court her.

Sarah teasingly promised to marry Polk only if he won a seat in the Tennessee legislature. After winning the election, Sarah and James were married on January 1, 1824. Although Sarah and James were unable to have children due to his childhood illnesses, they remained very close to his parents and nine siblings.

Polk continued his strong allegiance to Jackson, both personally and politically. Throughout his seven terms in the Tennessee House of Representatives, Polk worked tirelessly toward the goal of seeing Jackson elected president. In 1835, during his second term in the state legislature, Polk was selected to be the speaker of the House. In his earlier years in politics, the dominant party was the Democratic-Republicans. However, this party was falling apart, and Polk aligned himself with the future Democrats who supported farmers and workers, free public education and lower tariffs.

In 1836, the Whig party carried Tennessee in the presidential and gubernatorial elections. Desperate to have the Democrats governing his home state, Polk ran for and won the governor's race in 1839. After being defeated in two re-election campaigns, Polk believed his political career to be over, and he returned to his law practice.

The presidential election of 1844 began, and the nation had to choose its candidates. Controversy over the annexation of Texas became an issue. With Jackson and Polk supporting this territorial expansion, Polk, subsequently, became a dark-horse candidate. Opponents from the Whig party ran on the slogan "Who is James K. Polk?" They stressed the fact that few people had heard of him and that he had a boring personality. Polk won the presidential election in 1845 over Whig candidate Henry Clay by a very narrow margin.

The man who once believed his political life to be over was now the 13th president of the United States.

First Lady Sarah Childress Polk proved to be an excellent political wife. She was gracious and socially elegant but upheld her strict Presbyterian background. She banned wine, dancing and card playing in the White House. She also decreased formal entertaining in the president's house. President Polk was a very somber man of short stature by nature. Sarah was concerned that her unimposing husband was never noticed when entering a crowded room, so she introduced the idea of playing "Hail to the Chief" (a Scottish folk melody) to announce the president's arrival.

President Polk then set out to fulfill his campaign promises. He conducted lengthy negotiations with Great Britain over a part of the Northwest known as the Oregon Territory. In 1846, Polk successfully added the Oregon Territory to the United States. Polk was halfway to fulfilling his campaign promise of territorial expansion. Annexing Texas and California to the United States caused rebellion on two sides. The Mexican government refused to relinquish the lands north of the Rio Grande River. Congress was in a battle over annexing Texas, fearing it would become a slave state and upsetting the balance of slave and non-slave states.

In 1846, Polk decided to take on the Mexican government and declared war. He was the first U. S. president to function as commander in chief of the armed forces. Polk ran the war himself, working 18-hour days personally commanding his generals. By 1847, the U. S. troops captured Mexico City, bringing the war to an end. However, his victories in winning Texas and California and obtaining the Oregon Territory only caused more political unrest between the slave and non-slave states. Unable to find a solution to the question of whether to admit new states as free or slave, Polk chose to avoid the issue. This deep controversy forced Polk to decline running again for the presidency in 1848. Instead, he opted to retire.

Polk's excessive work habits literally put him in his grave. He was once quoted as saying, "No president who performs his duties faithfully and conscientiously can have any leisure." By the time he left office in 1848, his habit of working 12- to 18-hour days had lowered his immune system. It took a critical toll on his chronically frail body. Three months after leaving office he fell ill, possibly from a cholera outbreak while visiting New Orleans.

On July 15, 1849, Polk died at the age of 53. In his last will and testament, Polk requested that Sarah make provisions to free their slaves on her death. Sarah lived another 42 years.

President Harry Truman was quoted as saying, "James K. Polk, a great president, said what he intended to do and did it." Although most people know little of the details of the life and presidency of James Knox Polk, many historians still consider him one of the most successful presidents in U. S. history.

Zachary Taylor

Known as "Old Rough and Ready," Zachary Taylor was a living contradiction in many ways. General Taylor was definitely a strong commander. In 40 years of military service to the Union, he never considered defeat as an option, even when the odds were vastly against him. When he became president, he governed more like a military general accustomed to giving orders than as a political negotiator.

Born near Barboursville, VA, on November 24, 1784, Zachary was the third of eight children born to Richard and Sarah Dabney Strother Taylor. Both his mother and father came from wealthy Virginia families. Zachary grew up as a happy child on the 10,000-acre family plantation but never acquired a formal education, studying only the basics of reading and penmanship.

Zachary's father had served in the Revolutionary War, so it was only natural that Zachary join the U. S. Army. In 1808, at the age of 24, Zachary joined the military with the rank of lieutenant, thanks to his father's connections. Two years later, while holding the rank of captain, Zachary met and married Margaret "Peggy" Mackall Smith, who was the daughter of a wealthy Maryland family.

In the next few years, Peggy gave birth to five daughters and one son. Throughout 40 years of her husband's military service, Peggy and the children followed Zachary to the many outposts where he was stationed. She preferred the austere life of a military wife to the society life she had previously known. Tragically, Peggy and two of her daughters came down with malaria during this time on the frontier. Peggy survived, but two of their five daughters died, and Peggy's health was forever impaired.

Although a military leader, Taylor had a total disregard for the pomp and circumstance of an army officer. Even as a general, he was famous for his sloppy appearance. Taylor's willingness to share the hardships of life in the field alongside his men earned him the respect of his troops. General Taylor chewed tobacco and had a reputation for being a gifted spittoon marksman. This served him well later in life when the spittoon was on the luxurious carpet of the White House.

Artist Concept:

General Zachary Taylor was definitely a strong commander. In 40 years of military service to the Union, he never considered defeat as an option. Therefore, he is depicted as "Old Rough and Ready."

Sculptor: Lee Leuning | Benefactor: Stanford Adelstein

Taylor proved to be a fearless military leader. In the War of 1812, he defended Fort Harrison, a frontier outpost, with 50 soldiers against an army of 450 Native Americans. When President James Polk ordered Taylor to guard disputed lands near the Rio Grande River, a Mexican division of 6,000 soldiers attacked Taylor's command of 4,000 soldiers. He defeated them soundly, and his heroics elevated him to the rank of major general. In 1847, President Polk became jealous of Taylor's growing popularity and stripped Taylor of all but 5,000 men at an outpost in Mexico. Mexican General Santa Anna took advantage of Taylor's situation and attacked this small army with over 15,000 soldiers. Taylor stood his ground in the thick of the battle, fighting the Mexican army to a standstill. When the weary soldiers awoke the next morning, Santa Anna had retreated. General Taylor then retired to civilian life after an illustrious 40-year career as a military legend.

Around 1847, there was growing concern in balancing the amount of pro-slavery and anti-slavery states in the Union. With the election of a new president, the Whig party knew that their candidates would have to appease both sides. They believed that Zachary Taylor, a popular war hero and slave owner from the South, and Millard Fillmore, a neutral Northerner who didn't have a particular stand on anything, would be the perfect ticket for victory.

When the Whig party unanimously nominated Taylor for their presidential candidate in 1848, he was at his Baton Rouge, LA, plantation. A formal notification of his nomination was mailed to him in the common practice of the day—postage-due. Taylor had informed his local postmaster to stop delivering any postage-due mail, so his official nomination notification sat in the dead-letter office for weeks until the president of the convention realized what had happened and sent a second, pre-paid notice.

It seems contradictory that Taylor became a political figure at all since he had never had enough interest in the political workings of the country to vote! The first time he ever cast a ballot was for himself in the presidential election of 1848 when he was 64 years old.

Peggy Taylor was strongly opposed to Zachary's pursuit of the presidency. She had suffered through many years of separation due to wars and military assignments that put her husband in harm's way. She felt that his commitment to the preservation of the Union would consume what little time they had left together. It is said that she prayed every night that he would lose the presidential election so they could retire in comfort and solitude.

On November 7, 1848, the Taylor/Fillmore ticket was victorious. This strange matching of men was indeed a contradiction. "Rough and Ready" Taylor was viewed as a frontiersman, while the tall, stately and distinguished Fillmore cut a much more presidential appearance. Actually, it was only after the election that President Taylor met his new vice president. Having no previous acquaintance, their first meeting did not go well. Despite the fact that Fillmore had a much stronger political background, Taylor made it clear that he was making the decisions and relegated Fillmore to only the most minor of vice-presidential responsibilities.

With the entrance of new territories and statehood for large areas of the country,

Taylor saw his presidency being defined by keeping the Union and the Constitution strong. Although Taylor had been born into a family of slave owners and had slaves to work his own fields, his political stand contradicted his background. His 40 years of service in the military made him committed to the nation and not to special interests in the North or South. He believed that slaves were necessary for the economy of the country. He also felt that the Northern industrial states should remain free states.

He was passionate about preserving the Union and the Constitution at all costs. When the South accused him of being a traitor and threatened to secede from the Union, President Taylor angrily said that he would personally lead the troops himself to defend his cause. He even threatened to hang every traitor to the Union that he could get his hands on.

Quickly his dissenters were demanding a compromise to quiet this pending conflict. Senator Henry Clay introduced a new plan—the Compromise of 1850—in hopes of an acceptable compromise for all political interests. It included five points: California should be admitted to the Union as a free state; Texas's borders should be defined, and the territory of New Mexico established; the territory of Utah should be established; The Fugitive Slave Act, which allowed runaway slaves to be returned to the South, should be enacted; and, slave trade (not slavery itself) should be abolished in the District of Columbia.

President Taylor felt that the Compromise of 1850, presented in its all-or-nothing format would only inflame the conflicts between the North and the South. He also told Congress that unless California was allowed to enter the Union as a free state, he would oppose the entire Compromise. The battle waged on among the politicians, but a national tragedy ended the debate for a time. The Compromise of 1850 would have to wait, unsigned. On the Fourth of July, President Taylor chose to take an afternoon stroll on an especially hot day in Washington, D. C. Overtaken by the heat, he returned to the White House to enjoy a lunch of cherries and milk. By that evening, Taylor became violently ill, stricken by food poisoning from either the fruit or spoiled milk. Five days later, with his family at his side, he died on the evening of July 9, 1850, just 16 months after his inauguration. His wife, Peggy, was so stricken by his sudden death that she was unable to attend the president's funeral, and she died two years later at the home of her son still grieving her loss.

Educator Horace Mann once said this of Zachary Taylor: "He is a most simple-minded old man. He has the least show or pretension about him of any man I ever saw; talks as artlessly as a child about affairs of state, and does not seem to pretend to a knowledge of anything of which he is ignorant. He is a remarkable man in some respects; and it is remarkable that such a man should be President of the United States." He was a man of contradictions, indeed.

Millard Fillmore

History has not been kind to Millard Fillmore. Ranked among the bottom ten of the United States presidents, Fillmore is better known for his failures than his accomplishments in his political life. However, there are those who say that Fillmore was a man of political courage who was devoted to the Union and the Constitution. Because of that devotion, he lost a favorable place in history.

Millard Fillmore was the second vice president in American history to become president due to the death of his predecessor. President Zachary Taylor succumbed to food poisoning during a heat wave in Washington, D. C., in 1850, thrusting an ill-prepared Vice-President Fillmore into the presidency with the threat of civil war looming.

The second of nine children born to Nathaniel and Phoebe Fillmore on January 7, 1800, Millard was born in the log home on his parent's farm in Cayuga County, NY. As a child, he worked on his father's farm until the age of 14. He was self taught through the only books available to him—the family Bible, a hymnal and an almanac.

At the age of 14, he was an apprentice to a cloth maker. As an apprentice, he was financially bound to stay at this job but was treated so badly by the master of the mill that he bought off his apprenticeship and walked the 100 miles back home. As a result of the beatings he received from the master, he later wrote, "It made me feel for the weak and unprotected and to hate the insolent tyrant in every station in life." This bitter lesson was reflected later in Fillmore's life with his personal opposition of slavery and his work against the practice of debtors' prisons.

Upon his return home, he began work at a wool mill. Soon Millard was able to buy a dictionary, and he read the dictionary to improve his vocabulary as he walked between the mill machines. At the age of 19, Millard decided to take his education further and enrolled in New Hope Academy. It wasn't until then that Fillmore ever read a history of the United States or even saw a map of the country. At the academy, he filled in the gaps in his education with the help of a teacher, Abigail Powers. Through their mutual passion for books, Millard and Abigail (who was only one year older) fell in love and soon were engaged to be married.

Artist Concept:

Fillmore is depicted as a sullen, introverted man, and the sculptor chose to depict him with an expression of slight annoyance at visitors who interrupt his reading.

Sculptor: James Van Nuys | Benefactors: Richard and Tracy Perdue; Lori Stueber and sons, Reed and Riley Stueber

Rather than continue at the wool mills, Millard wanted to further himself and chose to study the law. After taking a teaching position to finance his law studies, Fillmore was admitted to the practice of law in New York state. Three years later, after establishing his own successful law firm in Buffalo, NY, he sent for Abigail, and they were married on February 5, 1826. Their son, Millard Powers Fillmore, was born in 1828 followed by the birth of a daughter, Mary Abigail Fillmore, in 1832.

By the time Fillmore was married, he had become very interested in politics. In 1828, Fillmore won a seat in the New York state legislature. Putting his new-found political position to use, he helped pass a law against putting people in jail for not paying their debts, and he helped pass a more lenient bankruptcy law.

In 1832, Fillmore was elected to the U. S. Congress. Andrew Jackson was president at that time, and a new party was being formed to oppose Jackson's policies. This anti-Jackson movement developed into the Whig Party, although it had not yet gained popularity. Fillmore returned to Buffalo where he worked behind the scenes to promote the Whig Party within his district. This enabled him to be elected to Congress again in 1836. In 1842, Fillmore returned to his New York law practice.

By 1847, Fillmore was elected to the powerful state financial position of comptroller of New York. This influential role brought him to the attention of the Whig Party who were searching for a vice-presidential candidate to run with Mexican-War-hero General Zachary Taylor. General Taylor was a slave owner from Louisiana, and the Whigs realized they needed a northerner who took a middle-of-the-road approach to slavery. One popular history book was more succinct in its explanation: "Fillmore was put on the Whig ticket . . . primarily because he was so dull."

In a close victory over a Democratic candidate in 1848, President Taylor and Vice-President Fillmore were headed for the White House. Strange as it may seem, Taylor and Fillmore had not even met until after they were sworn into office. Frontiersman "Rough and Ready" Taylor was a strong contrast to the tall, well-dressed and well-spoken Fillmore. Although Fillmore had a strong background in politics, President Taylor never asked for his advice.

As vice president, Fillmore had few duties other than presiding over the Senate. This was a difficult time in the history of the nation, as the Union was being threatened by civil war over the division of pro- and anti-slavery states. Debates were flying from both sides over the Compromise of 1850, attempting to reconcile pro- and anti-slavery movements, abolishing the selling of slaves in Washington, D. C., and allowing the capture and return of runaway slaves to their southern masters. President Taylor was opposed to the Compromise, but Fillmore believed in the Union and the Constitution and told the president that he would vote in favor of the Compromise if there was a tie in the Senate.

On a hot Fourth of July in Washington, D. C., history made a sharp turn for the country and changed the life of Fillmore forever. While lunching on fresh fruit and spoiled milk,

President Taylor contracted food poisoning and died in his sleep just 16 months into his presidency on July 9, 1850.

President Fillmore took the oath of office on July 10, 1850, and immediately pursued the passing of the Compromise of 1850. He sincerely believed his support for the bill kept the Union from falling apart. Fillmore dispatched Commodore Matthew Perry to Japan to establish trade agreements with the Pacific Rim. The president then began to improve the nation's transportation systems, funding better railroads, waterways and harbors. These have been noted as Fillmore's most lasting achievements.

After becoming president, Fillmore decided that he needed a new carriage befitting his role as the head of his country. A White House servant soon found a bargain and invited the president to inspect it. The president asked, "This is all very well, but how would it do for the president of the United States to ride around in a second-hand carriage?" The servant replied, "But surely, your Excellency is only a second-hand president."

Due to his stand on the Compromise of 1850, Fillmore recognized that re-election was not possible. By signing the Fugitive Slave Act, he lost the support of the northern Whig Party, and so he left the presidency at the end of his first term in 1853. Sadly, his beloved Abigail, who had been in poor health most of her adult life, died from pneumonia contracted while attending the inaugural speech of Fillmore's successor, Franklin Pierce. His daughter, Mary Abigail, who served as hostess at her father's side during White House ceremonies, died of cholera one year later. Fillmore lost his presidency and two of the most important people in his life.

In 1855, while visiting Oxford University, ex-President Fillmore was offered an honorary degree. Coming from such humble beginnings and illiteracy, it was believed this would be a great honor for him. However, upon learning that the degree was written in Latin, Fillmore modestly declined. He said, "I had not the advantage of a classical education and no man should, in my judgment, accept a degree he cannot read."

When returning to private life, Fillmore wasn't ready to quit politics and, lacking the support of his old political party, joined the American or "Know-Nothing" Party. This party was called this because, whenever members were asked about its organization, they replied, "I know nothing." In fact, the American Party was opposed to immigration and was anti-Catholic. In 1856, Fillmore again made a bid for the White House but lost.

Fillmore quietly retired to Buffalo where he married a wealthy widow, Caroline Carmichael. He remained in hearty health until stricken with a stroke in February 1874. Several weeks later, he suffered a second stroke and died in his sleep on March 8, 1874, at the age of 74. Fillmore was eulogized by President Ulysses S. Grant. He said, "The long-continued and useful public service and eminent purity of character of the deceased ex-President will be remembered."

Franklin Pierce

Franklin Pierce (pronounced "purse" by the family) was born with the proverbial silver political spoon in his mouth. His father, Benjamin Pierce, fought victoriously in the American Revolution and became a farmer, tavern keeper, leader of the Democrat-Republican Party in New Hampshire and governor of New Hampshire.

Franklin was born on November 23, 1804, in a log cabin on the banks of the Contoocook River of Hillsborough County, NH. He was one of eight children. Although the family was by no means wealthy, Benjamin and Anna Pierce wanted their children to have a better education than their own and sent him to private schools. Franklin was an active and devilish youngster—quick to pick a fight or pull a prank. He was a bright student, and, according to legend, often spent his recess time tutoring slow learners.

Portrait by George Healy

At 15, he entered Bowdoin College where his college mates included Henry Wadsworth Longfellow and Nathaniel Hawthorne. Hawthorne was a shy, incoming freshman, and they became lifelong friends despite differing personalities. A thunder and lightning storm brought Franklin and another fellow student, Jane Appleton, together. Jane was rushing across the Bowdoin College campus when she got caught in the storm and crouched in terror under a tree. He picked her up and carried her to safety. This encounter led to romance and eventually marriage. Franklin graduated from college in 1824 at 19, ranking third in his class.

Pierce began studying law after college and was admitted to the bar in 1827. He then opened a law office in Hillsboro. Following in his father's political footsteps, 24-year-old Franklin won a seat in the legislature. He was re-elected three times and became speaker of the lower house at the age of 26. In 1828, Pierce was elected to Congress.

On November 19, 1834, Pierce married Jane Means Appleton just before his 30th birthday, and they had three sons—two of which died in infancy. She doted on their third son, Benjamin. Outgoing and personable, Pierce loved politics and had great success as

Artist Concept:

Historians do not consider Pierce to have been a great (or even a good) president. He had a tragic life, and the fact he was able to fulfill his presidential obligations at all seems worthy of admiration. The artist captures the sad, haunted look that comes through so clearly in historic photographs of him.

Sculptor: James Van Nuys | Benefactor: Ludwick Trust

a congressman and senator. Jane was just the opposite. She was reserved and shy. The daughter of a somber minister, she was fiercely religious and committed devotee of the temperance movement.

Pierce's political career accelerated when he was elected to the Senate in 1836, but life in Washington took its toll on him. Jean didn't accompany Pierce when he returned to Washington in 1836 because she suffered from tuberculosis and strongly disliked the "dirty politics" in the nation's capital. In the 1830s, the city was an unpleasant place. Politicians lived mostly in shabby boardinghouses. Pierce proceeded to live a rowdy lifestyle with other bachelor congressmen and often drank more than he should—a vice he carried for the rest of his life. As a result, Jane constantly nagged him to give up his political career. He finally decided to retire from the Senate in 1842 and returned to New Hampshire.

Wanting to follow in his father's military footsteps, Pierce signed up to fight in the Mexican War in 1847. During the Battle of Contreras, Pierce was injured when his horse fell, resulting in a serious groin injury that caused him to faint from the pain. The following day, he fainted again in front of his troops, which later resulted in political challengers calling him a coward and "fainting general." Pierce returned home in 1848 as a brigadier general.

In 1852, Pierce and his friends began planning to obtain the Democratic presidential nomination. James Buchanan and Lewis Cass were vying for the nomination, but there was not a clear majority winner after 35 ballots were cast. Pierce's friends believed he offered something for everyone and that he had all the qualities of the presidential tradition. He was born in a log cabin, was a member of a patriotic family, had a military record and had served in the legislature and Congress. They entered his name on the 36th ballot, and, by the 49th ballot, the entire convention agreed that Pierce could unite the opposing factions of the party. Jane did not know that her husband was secretly seeking his party's nomination for president, and she fainted with horrified shock when she heard that he had been nominated. Pierce won the presidential election in 1852 in a landslide over Whig-Party candidate Winfield Scott.

Pierce carried the personal tragedies that historians believe destroyed his confidence in himself to be a good president. The loss of two sons, the debilitating illness of his wife and his conflicting feelings of being able to serve as president all took their toll. To make matters worse, the Pierce's 11-year-old son, Benjamin, died when their railroad car toppled off the tracks on their way to Washington, D. C., for Pierce to take office. Mrs. Pierce believed God had taken their son so that Pierce would not be distracted from his presidential duties. Pierce carried the guilt for his son's death, and his grieving wife did not attend his inauguration or take part in White House affairs for two years.

Known as a brilliant orator, 48-year-old Pierce delivered his inaugural address from memory without notes. He said, "It is a relief to feel that no heart but my own can know the personal regret and bitter sorrow over which I have been borne to a position so suitable for others rather than desirable for myself."

Most historians rank Pierce as one of the worst presidents to serve this country.

Nothing of historic significance happened during his term in office due to his lack of commitment and indecisiveness. His opposing party, the Whigs, portrayed Pierce as "the fainting general" and a confirmed drunk with a "do-nothing Congress." One of the few notable acts signed by President Pierce was the Kansas-Nebraska Act, which allowed residents of the territories to decide whether their regions were "slave" or "free." This act did not satisfy either side of this divisive issue. Civil war lurked on the horizon, but Pierce would not (or could not) resolve the issues of slavery, and the results were disastrous. Kansas broke out in a bitter, bloody conflict. What the nation needed was not a bid for popularity but a strong, decisive leader. Pierce proved to be unable to rise to the task at hand. He had the dubious distinction of failing to receive his own party's endorsement for re-election and was replaced by James Buchanan as his party's candidate.

Jane Appleton Pierce.

Even his lifelong friend, Hawthorne, would not have described Pierce as a sturdy man. He suffered prolonged bouts of depression believed to have been brought on by a constant battle he waged with himself over whether or not he deserved his success.

Pierce and his wife lived in the White House frugally, saving about half of his $25,000 annual salary, which allowed them to live comfortably after retirement. After their Washington years, the Pierces travelled in Europe and the West Indies. Jane and his best friend, Hawthorne, died in 1863 and 1864, respectively, and Pierce found himself all alone. He found solace in the bottle and died a bitter man on October 8, 1869, at the age of 64.

James Buchanan

James Buchanan, Jr., was born in a log cabin in Cove Gap, PA, on April 23, 1791, to James and Elizabeth Buchanan, who were both of Scots-Irish descent. James was the second of 11 children. At the age of five, the family moved to Mercersburg where his father was a successful farmer and merchant. His mother had no formal education but was well-read, teaching her children the works of Milton and Pope. When James was old enough, he went to work in his father's store, keeping his father's books and accounts.

White House Historical Association
Portrait by George Healy

James had a habit of holding his head cocked to the left, a posture he developed to compensate for a rare eye disorder that left him nearsighted in one eye and farsighted in the other. Depending on whether he wished to focus on something close or at a distance, he would close one eye, cock his head and look from a single eye. Many described him as a large, quizzical bird. He apparently coped well with his disorder, being an avid reader and not wearing glasses until late in life.

James, Jr., loved and feared his father because James, Sr., was a stern taskmaster. He assigned his son chores that were well beyond his ability and critical of young James' performances. James rarely experienced the feeling of a task well done. In his later years, James regretted that his father never lived to see him rise to the highest office in the nation.

At the age of 16, James entered Dickinson College. His mother wanted him to study for the ministry, but his father felt that James would better serve the growing family business interest by studying law. James proved to be a good student, but when he was away from his father's stern hand, he engaged in rowdy escapades and drinking bouts with his fellow classmates. This resulted in James's expulsion at the end of his first year of college. Because of his father's influence and James's promise to toe the line, he was readmitted. Holding to this promise, he graduated with honors the following year at the age of 18. He moved to Lancaster, studied law under a local attorney and opened his own practice three years later.

In August 1814, Buchanan thought that running for the state assembly would attract

Artist Concept:

To portray Buchanan's impotent presidency, he is depicted standing with hands clasped behind his back, perhaps holding papers that suggest a policy or executive order considered but never implemented. Note his trademark high collar, the voluminous trousers and his head inclined slightly to the left, as was his habit.

Sculptor: James Michael Maher | Benefactors: Charles and Mary Jane Wendt

more clients. When news that the British were burning Washington reached Lancaster, Buchanan realized he would have to show his patriotism if he wished to be elected. He joined a local militia company and marched off to Baltimore, MD, which was the next British target. Luckily, his unit did not see action, and Buchanan returned to Lancaster in time to win the legislative seat.

In 1818, at the age of 27, Buchanan fell in love with Ann Coleman, who was the daughter of a wealthy iron-mill owner. Ann was a beautiful, affectionate, petulant and wild child. Many believed she may have been emotionally unstable. Ann's parents opposed her relationship with James because they believed him to be a fortune hunter, but Buchanan was wealthy in his own right due to his law practice. He was rumored to have been worth over $250,000 by the age of 30. Despite her parents' disapproval, Ann and James became engaged in the summer of 1819.

However, rumors began to surface that Buchanan was seen with another woman. The couple quarreled, and Ann broke off the engagement, moving to Philadelphia to stay with relatives. Shortly after she moved, Ann died under mysterious circumstances, possibly suicide. Her doctor said that this was "the first instance he ever knew of hysteria producing death." The Coleman family was so bitter toward Buchanan that they would not allow him to attend Ann's funeral. Buchanan kept his vow to never marry, and he became the only bachelor to become president.

A grieving Buchanan returned to politics and was elected to Congress in 1820. In 1832, President Andrew Jackson sent him to Russia as U. S. minister, but the politically ambitious Buchanan did not want to be away from the U. S. too long. He soon returned and was elected to the Senate in 1834, serving for the next 11 years there.

Buchanan loved and lived by the Constitution. He believed that he could do only what the Constitution explicitly stated. Because the Constitution allowed slavery, he politically tolerated it but personally opposed it. Buchanan once bought slaves in Washington, D. C., and took them back to Pennsylvania and set them free.

It had been Buchanan's lifelong dream to become president, wanting to serve in the manner of heroes like George Washington. On his first bid for a presidential nomination in 1848, he failed to win and returned to Wheatland. In 1852, he again narrowly missed the Democratic nomination. At the age of 62, he was given a diplomatic mission as U. S. minister to Great Britain. At the Democratic National Convention in 1856, 65-year-old Buchanan won his party's nomination and went on to finally win the presidency.

Having never married, Buchanan chose to have his niece, Harriet Lane, accompany him to Washington to serve as his hostess in the White House. The three previous first ladies, due to personal tragedies and religious beliefs, had little desire to participate in the pomp and circumstance of the White House. Harriet was a refreshing change to the activities of her uncle's presidency. A lavish inaugural ball was the first of many galas held at the White House, and Harriet's outgoing personality, poise and enthusiasm made her very popular. Women even copied her fashionable low-cut dresses and frivolous hats.

Buchanan was meticulous about trivial matters. He recorded his expenditures daily, including pennies spent by his valet for pins and suspender buttons. He once refused to accept a check for $15,000 because it was short ten cents.

History ranks Buchanan as one of the worst presidents. Like his predecessor, Franklin Pierce, he lacked the conviction or strength to make critical decisions facing the nation. He did not comprehend the depth of feelings on both sides of the slavery question. He despised abolitionists and saw little injustice in slavery, claiming the slaves were treated with kindness and humanity.

In 1859, during the last part of Buchanan's presidency, violence accelerated between slave owners and abolitionists. John Brown's raid at Harper's Ferry brought national attention to the emotional divisions concerning slavery. The Supreme Court handed down the Dred Scott decision, which supported Buchanan's view that slavery was rooted in the Constitution and could not be legislated out of existence, freeing him from making a critical decision about the Union. Buchanan believed that the federal government did not have the Constitutional authority to force any state to remain in the Union, and, therefore, it was not the president's responsibility to act. Before he left office, seven Southern states had withdrawn from the Union. When he left office, the country was fractured far beyond any compromise.

With great relief, Buchanan left the White House, leaving a letter for Abraham Lincoln, which said, "My dear sir, If you are as happy in entering the White House as I shall feel returning to Wheatland, you are a happy man indeed."

Buchanan returned home a scorned man. He spent the rest of his life defending himself against accusations that his unwillingness to act against the South had helped bring on the Civil War. On June 1, 1868, Buchanan died at the age of 76. Shortly before his death, he told a friend, "I have no regret for any public act of my life, and history will vindicate my memory." His faith was misplaced, however. History still bears a grudge.

U.S. Marines attack John Brown's "fort" at Harper's Ferry, which is an example of violence that Buchanan failed to stop.

Abraham Lincoln

Abraham Lincoln's political accomplishments are legend. Most Americans are familiar with his role in the Civil War, his Emancipation Proclamation to free the slaves, the Lincoln-Douglas debates and his ability to appeal to the nation's best ideals while acting "with malice towards none." These accomplishments made him the most popular and beloved president in American history. However, it also made some hate him just as much.

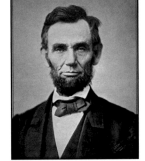

Born in a dirt-floor, one-room log cabin on February 12, 1809, Abe rose from the backwoods of Hardin County, KY, to the White House. Abe's father, Thomas, was a farmer and a carpenter who could neither read nor write. He was only able to sign his name. His mother, Nancy Hanks Lincoln, was also illiterate but was loving to her children, Sarah and Abraham. (Another son, Thomas, died in infancy). Lincoln once said, "All I am or hope to be, I owe to my sainted mother." However, Nancy died at 34 of "milk sickness" when Abe was just nine years old. One year after his wife's death, Thomas married Sarah Bush Johnston, a widow with three children. Although Abraham was never close to his father, he instantly took a liking to his stepmother because she was very kind to him and encouraged his education.

As a frontier young man, Abe did his share of plowing, clearing and planting. His father sometimes hired him out to neighboring farms. Abe became an expert with an ax and was a skilled rail-splitter. He was also known to be a real scrapper, challenging neighboring young men to wrestle. His 6'4", 180-pound body with gangling arms and legs and sunken chest made him a formidable opponent. His strength from swinging an ax and splitting rails made him a winner in most matches.

Abe estimated that he had approximately 18 months of formal education from itinerant teachers passing through town and stopping by to give a few lessons. Once he learned to read, Abe became a voracious reader, studying the family Bible and often walking miles to neighbors' homes to borrow books. "My best friend," he once said, "is the man

Artist Concept:

This work gives an insight into the burdens that Lincoln bore during his presidency. He is depicted holding a telegram from the front lines, which informs him of the casualties of so many sons. Lincoln reflects on the cost of war while his own innocent son plays with a toy cannon at his feet.

Sculptor: James Michael Maher | Benefactors: Melba Hall and sons Fred, Pat, Mike and Bill

who'll git me a book I ain't read." Abe went from an illiterate young child to an admirer of Shakespeare. He especially enjoyed Macbeth and Hamlet, reciting whole passages from memory.

Surprisingly, Lincoln was an intensely brooding person, who was plagued with chronic depression. His speeches, letters and conversations were filled with death, almost as if he was obsessed by it. He also feared losing his mind and worried about his own sanity. He was very superstitious, looking for signs and visions and believing that dreams were the omens of coming events. Lincoln actually had a dream in which he witnessed his own death, seeing the weeping mourners as his train traveled across the country.

He often used humor to make a point with folksy tales and bawdy stories. His stories usually poked fun at himself. Lincoln was once called "two-faced" by a rival. Lincoln responded, "If I had another face, do you think I'd wear this one?"

Of Note: **Lincoln looking at the war report.**

At the age of 21, Lincoln struck out on his own and settled in New Salem, IL, where he worked as a clerk in a general store for $15 a month. Two years later, President Andrew Jackson appointed Lincoln to be postmaster of New Salem at a wage of $55 a month. He was required to be accountable for postal receipts, and he kept them in an old blue sock hidden in a wooden chest. In conducting his postal responsibilities, Lincoln stuffed the mail into his stove-pipe hat and walked miles to neighbors' homes in his district. Working with the public, Lincoln developed social skills and honed his down-home, story-telling skills. Upon leaving his postmaster position, Lincoln produced the blue sock with his revenues balanced to the penny.

In 1836, Lincoln was elected to four terms in the Illinois legislature. Lincoln's campaign skills greatly impressed the leader of the Whig Party, John Todd Stuart. Stuart was a successful lawyer in Springfield and encouraged Lincoln to study law. Lincoln mastered every law book he could buy or borrow. He received his license to practice law, moved to Springfield and became Stuart's law partner.

In 1839, Lincoln began courting Mary Todd. She was barely 21, having just moved from Lexington, KY, when she first met Lincoln. Her wealthy, aristocratic family did not approve of the poor, self-made Lincoln. She had been raised in a 14-room mansion; he in a log cabin. She was privately tutored in dance, drama, music and French; he was self-taught. After an on-and-off again courtship (including a broken engagement), Abe, 33, married Mary Todd, 23, on November 4, 1842. Lincoln was elected to the U. S. House of Representatives in 1847.

The newlyweds spent their first year of marriage living in a boarding house where their first child, Robert, was born in 1843. They later moved to a small wood-frame cottage at 214 S. Fourth Street which was the only home the couple ever owned. In 1846, a second son, Edward, was born but died four years later. The untimely death of their beloved son was only the beginning of the challenges the Lincoln family would bear.

Their third son, William "Willie" Wallace Lincoln, was born in 1850. Willie and his older brother, Robert, were inseparable. Born in April 1853, Thomas "Tad" Lincoln was the youngest child in the family. He proved to be a handful for his family because he was developmentally disabled or hyperactive. He was slow to learn and spoke with a lisp. At eight years old, he still could not dress himself. His behavior became so erratic that Mrs. Lincoln hired a nurse for him. Despite having tutors, Tad was still unable to read or write at twelve years old.

In 1860, at the Republican National Convention, Lincoln became the party's presidential nominee. He was elected president of the United States in 1860 and re-elected in 1864.

Mary had a sparkling personality and wit that made her quite popular. However, she also had an explosive temper, was jealous of those close to her husband and was paranoid and irrational. Actually, it was determined that she was mentally unstable. When she became first lady, newspapers described her as plump and plain. Considering these reports to be an insult to her and her husband, she went on spending sprees that totaled $27,000 by 1864. She indulged herself with money her husband could not afford, adding to the ridicule she faced from the public and the media. At a time when women were supposed to be soft-spoken and demure, Mrs. Lincoln spoke her mind on political matters so forcefully that her husband's staff referred to her as the "hellcat."

Tragedy struck the Lincoln family again in 1862 when 11-year-old Willie suddenly became ill with typhoid fever and died in the White House. (He was the only child of a president to die there). Wildly distraught, Mrs. Lincoln sought out spiritualists to contact her dead son, only to be bilked out of another small fortune. In fact, Willie's death seemed to have been the breaking point for her.

Shortly after beginning his second presidential term, Lincoln found his wife in a particularly foul mood one day and decided to appease her by offering her an evening at the theatre on April 14, 1865. Two productions were being shown that night—*Aladdin! or the Wonderful Lamp!* at Grover's Theatre and *Our American Cousin* at Ford's Theatre. The president wanted to attend the Grover's Theatre production with Tad but gave in to Mrs. Lincoln's pleas to go to Ford's Theatre where they could be seen by the public in their grand presidential box. Actor and assassin John Wilkes Booth shot the president in the back of the head at a specific moment of the play when Booth knew the audience's laughter would drown out the shot. Lincoln was then taken across the street to a home where he died the next day. The funeral that followed was hauntingly similar to the dream that Lincoln had described so vividly just weeks before.

Booth was a deranged, Southern sympathizer, who was blinded by hate as the result of the Civil War. He silenced the man who had kept a nation united against all adversity. Abraham Lincoln was a man of humble beginnings who died a national treasure.

Andrew Johnson

If ever there was a man who was least likely to become president of the United States, it was Andrew Johnson. He had never been to school a day in his life and never mastered the basics of reading, grammar or math until he married at the age of 17. Once, he had a price on his head for running away from his employer before completing his indentured apprenticeship. Although he was born in the traditional log cabin, he was born to illiterate parents living in stark poverty. He didn't follow any religion. Despite all this, he did rise to the highest position in the land, grossly ill-equipped to serve the nation at a time when presidential leadership was critical.

Generally considered the worst president in American history, Johnson carried a heavy burden as the man who took over after the assassination of one of America's most loved presidents, Abraham Lincoln. His favorite pastimes were attending minstrel shows and going to the circus. He was prone to drunkenness (even appearing drunk at Lincoln's inauguration) and racism. He was the first U. S. president to be impeached.

That being said, Johnson served his country in the way he felt would best serve the Union by keeping the country united. Johnson was a pro-slavery Southern Democrat, serving as vice president to Republican President Lincoln. He fought equally hard against the secession of Southern states from the Union and against freeing of slaves as dictated by the Emancipation Proclamation.

Andrew was born on December 29, 1808, in Raleigh, NC. His father, Jacob, scratched out a living as a hotel porter and bank janitor. When Andrew was only three, his father died while trying to save two of his wealthy employers from drowning. His widowed mother, Mary "Polly" Johnson, took in work as a weaver and washerwoman to feed Andrew and his older brother, William.

A few years later, Polly married Turner Daugherty. Her new husband was just another mouth to feed, and the family's finances became even worse. When Andrew was 14, his parents apprenticed their two boys to a local tailor, James Selby. The boys were indentured servants, bound by law to work for Selby in return for food and clothing and teaching them the tailoring trade. After two years, the Johnson brothers ran away, breaking their contract.

Artist Concept:

When Johnson became president, he gave the whites of the South most of what they wanted in terms of power and privilege and had little sympathy for the plight of the freed slaves. Thus, his head is turned toward his left hand, which holds the southern half of the U. S. map.
Sculptor: James Van Nuys | Benefactors: The Bradsky Family

Selby ran an ad in the *Raleigh Gazette*, placing a reward of $10 for the delivery of William and Andrew Johnson back to him. Andrew fled to Carthage, NC, which was 75 miles south of Raleigh where he supported himself by tailoring. A year later, in 1826, he returned to Raleigh, gathered his mother and stepfather, crammed all their belongings into a one-horse cart and settled in Greeneville, TN. Andrew learned that the town tailor was retiring and opened his own shop under the sign "A. Johnson, Tailor" at 17.

The young tailor had tried to educate himself to no avail until he met his future wife, 16-year-old Eliza McCardle. The daughter of the village shoemaker, Eliza first spotted Andrew when he arrived in town with his ragtag family. She told a friend that it was "love at first sight." Eliza had lost her father when she was a small child, so she and Andrew developed a friendship based on their similar pasts. The friendship grew into a romance, and 18-year-old Andrew married Eliza at the home of the bride's mother on May 17, 1827.

It was a great match for Andrew because Eliza, though only a young girl herself, was well educated and could handle money well. While he sewed in his tailor shop, Eliza read to him and taught him to spell and write. She also taught him how to invest his money wisely. The Johnsons had five children, including one son who was killed serving as a Union soldier in the Civil War. At 16, Eliza Johnson married at a younger age than any other first lady. Shortly before Johnson took office as president, Eliza contracted tuberculosis and was confined to her bedroom in the White House throughout his presidency.

In 1828, at the age of 19, this hard-working, serious young tailor had greatly impressed the townspeople, and he was elected to the village council. Two years later, Johnson was voted mayor of Greeneville, identifying with the town's laboring class. Johnson liked politics, and he found that his common-man, tell-it-like-it-is style went over well with both the town's untrained laborers and skilled workers.

His popularity won him election to the state legislature in 1834 and 1838 and a seat in the state senate in 1841. From 1843 to 1853, 34-year-old Johnson served four terms in the U. S. House of Representatives as a Democrat. When his district was redrawn following the census of 1850, Johnson lost his seat in the House. He then ran for and won the election for governor of Tennessee from 1853 to 1857. Embracing his poverty-ridden beginnings, Governor Johnson still tailored his own clothes and once made a suit for the governor of Kentucky as a gesture of friendship.

In 1860, Abraham Lincoln, a simple man from Illinois, was elected to the presidency of the U. S.

When the Civil War broke out in 1861, Johnson was serving as a U. S. senator from the state of Tennessee. Being a senator from a Southern state, many believed that he would side with the secessionists, encouraging Southern slave states to leave the Union. To the contrary, Johnson denounced the secessionist movement and declared his intention to remain loyal to the Union. Of the secessionists, he said, "I would have them arrested and tried for treason, and, if convicted by the eternal God, they should suffer the penalty of the law at the hands of the executioner."

Andrew Johnson

When Tennessee joined the Confederacy, Johnson made good on his word, remaining in Washington to be hailed as a patriot in the North and deemed a traitor and hung in effigy in his hometown. His properties were confiscated, and his wife and two daughters were driven from the state with little more than what they could carry in a wagon. In 1862, after Northern troops had seized western and central Tennessee, Lincoln appointed Johnson as military governor of the state. He proved a fair-minded, able administrator, granting amnesty to former Confederate sympathizers.

When re-elected to a second term in 1864, Lincoln felt he needed a man like Southerner Johnson to balance the ticket. Together, the two won a sweeping victory over the Democratic candidate. One reporter from the *New York World* who was less than happy with Lincoln's choice for vice president said, "To think that one frail life stands between this insolent, clownish creature and the presidency! May God bless and spare Abraham Lincoln!"

Tragically, Lincoln was assassinated 41 days after the beginning of his second term. Had the assassin's plot gone as planned, Johnson would have been killed as well. Instead, he became president. During the first eight months of his term, Johnson took advantage of Congress being in recess and rushed through his own policies for the reconstruction of a divided nation. It quickly became clear that Johnson would block efforts to guarantee full equality for slaves. When Congress returned, Republicans passed bills to provide shelter and provisions for former slaves, protect slaves' rights in court and define all persons born in the U. S. as citizens. Johnson vetoed it all, but he was overridden. In a final humiliating gesture, the president was stripped of the power to override programs to enforce political and social rights for Southern slaves.

Furious, Johnson went straight to the people to regain his authority as president. However, his earlier abilities to reach the common man gave way to speeches full of vile, racist and abusive language. On several occasions, it appeared that the president had had too much to drink. In blatant defiance of the Tenure of Office Act, which stripped the president's authority to remove federal officials without Senate approval, Johnson fired Secretary of War Edwin Stanton.

Having lost support from Congress and the people, Johnson was finished. Congress voted to impeach Johnson by a vote of 126 to 47, charging that he had brought disgrace and ridicule on them. By a margin of one vote, the Senate voted not to convict Johnson, and he served the duration of the term won by Lincoln.

In 1875, Johnson returned to the Senate, becoming the only U. S. president to serve in that capacity after a presidential term. Johnson was quoted as saying, ". . . Thank God for the vindication." Johnson died on July 31, 1875, from a stroke and was buried on his own land outside of Greeneville. At his request, he was wrapped in the American flag with his head resting on a copy of the Constitution. Blinded by his personal sense of self-grandiosity, his bull-headed disregard for political reality and his blatant racism, Johnson greatly undermined the office of the presidency. One can only sadly speculate how different America would have been had Lincoln lived.

Ulysses S. Grant

American Civil War
Battle History

Belmont 1861

Fort Henry 1862

Fort Donelson 1862

Shiloh 1862

Vicksburg Campaign . . . 1862-63

Chattanooga 1863

Overland Campaign 1864

Petersburg Campaign . . 1864-65

Appomattox Surrender . . 1865

Ulysses S. Grant

Birth - 1822   Death - 1885
18th President of the United States
1869-1877.

A gift to The City of Presidents
In loving memory of our parents
A. C. "Bud" and Blanche Throstenson.

John Lopez, Sculptor

Ulysses S. Grant

President Ulysses S. Grant was somewhat of an enigma in American history. He was soft-spoken, shy and quiet, yet he was able to inspire great bravery from his soldiers on the battlefield. He was a man of honor who was unable or unwilling to see dishonor in others. He is best known as the Union general who led the North to victory over the Confederate South during the Civil War, but he was considered weak and ineffective as a president.

Hiram Ulysses Grant was born in a two-room cabin on April 27, 1822, in Point Pleasant, OH, and was the first of six children born to Jesse Root Grant and Hanna Simpson Grant. His parents were religious, hard-working people, and his father was a successful tanner.

Ulysses was a small, sensitive and quiet boy. When attending school, he was often bored and inattentive. The other school children took his subdued behavior for stupidity, nicknaming him "Useless." From an early age, he had a talent for handling horses so his father gave him that responsibility on the family farm. Eventually, Ulysses became known in the area for being able to manage unruly horses.

From 1836 to 1837, Ulysses attended Maysville (Kentucky) Seminary where he was on the debating team. In 1838, he attended the Presbyterian Academy at Ripley, OH, where he was an above-average student.

Grant's father recognized his son's ambition to further himself beyond the tanner business. The family could not afford a college education for any of their six children, but the U. S. Military Academy at West Point offered a superior free education in return for army service after graduating. Without telling Ulysses, Jesse appealed to Representative Thomas L. Hamer to appoint him to West Point. When he was informed that he had been accepted, Ulysses was terrified at the news, fearing that he would fail. With his father's encouragement, 17-year-old Grant decided to attend the school to take advantage of the education being offered to him.

When his congressman applied for Grant's appointment to West Point, he erroneously wrote his name as Ulysses S. Grant instead of Hiram Ulysses Grant. When Grant realized that his initials would be used on all his personal property at the academy, he decided that U.S.G. would look better than H.U.G and, thereafter, was known as Ulysses S. Grant.

Artist Concept:

Grant is depicted as one of our nation's most famous generals. His blue uniform and silver sword give this piece an authentic Civil War look. Grant was seldom seen without a cigar, and so one is included here. He has his right hand stretched out on a pedestal listing his Civil War battle history.

Sculptor: John Lopez | Benefactors: Paul Thorstenson Family

West Point proved difficult for a tanner's son with a limited education. However, his skill with horses was unmatched, and he set records in horseback riding. He was sure that he would be appointed a coveted spot in the army's cavalry, but he was assigned to the infantry after graduating in 1843, ranking 21st in a class of 39.

Grant's first assignment after West Point was the Fourth Infantry at the Jefferson Barracks in Missouri. His West Point roommate, Frederick Dent, lived nearby, and Dent often invited Grant to visit the family home. On one of these visits, Grant met Frederick's sister, Julia. She was short, plump, cross-eyed and socially pleasant, but Grant fell in love immediately. He took Julia on a buggy ride where they came to a flooded bridge. Julia was fearful of crossing the bridge, but Grant assured her it was safe. She grabbed his arm, warning, "I'm going to cling to you no matter what happens." After successfully crossing the bridge, Grant turned to her and asked, "How would you like to cling to me for the rest of your life?" Julia accepted the proposal and began a four-year engagement during which they saw each other only once.

Grant was a professional soldier, rising from second lieutenant to general. He fought in the Mexican War from 1846 to 1848, in which the young lieutenant was twice cited for his bravery. However, Grant found no glory in the ideals of war. He mourned the loss of his fellow soldiers and the devastation that the war created.

When the Mexican War ended, Ulysses and Julia were married on August 22, 1848, at the bride's home in St. Louis, MO. Little did the groom know that all three of his Southern attendants would fight against him as Confederates during the Civil War. The army then transferred Grant to distant locations in the Pacific Northwest and Oregon Territory—places he could not take Julia and their four children. He hated being separated from them. He fell into a deep depression, began drinking heavily and resigned suddenly from the army in 1854. Some historians believe that he was forced to resign his commission or be court-martialed because of his drinking.

Grant also loved smoking. He originally smoked a pipe, but when a war correspondent described him with a cigar in his teeth, people from all over the country sent him some 10,000 cigars. He had a habit of smoking 20 cigars a day—a habit that likely contributed to the mouth cancer he developed in later years.

Of Note: **Grant's cigar.**

Returning to his wife and children, 32-year-old Grant took up farming with limited success. He attempted several other lines of work, including selling wood, dealing in real estate and ultimately ended up clerking in his father's leather goods store. One Christmas, he even pawned his watch for $22 to buy presents for his family.

In 1861, the Civil War begun, and the North needed experienced army officers. The governor of Illinois appointed Grant to lead a volunteer regiment that no one else had been able to train. For this military position, he received three dollars a day. Grant grilled the men and instituted discipline, winning the men's respect and allegiance. President Abraham

Lincoln grew frustrated with his other overcautious officers who fought, not to win, but to avoid losing. Lincoln decided that Grant would be the man to lead the North to victory.

As commander of the Missouri district, he captured Fort Donelson, TN, in February 1862. This was the Union's first major victory and set the scene for Grant's rising national reputation. It was there that he gave his famous ultimatum to Confederate General Simon Buckner: "No terms except an unconditional and immediate surrender can be accepted." This earned him the nickname "Unconditional Surrender Grant" (U. S. Grant). Grant continued to win battles throughout the South, culminating in the surrender of General Robert E. Lee at Appomattox in 1865. In July 1866, Grant was promoted to general of the army—the first commander since Washington to hold that rank. In four years, Grant went from a leather-shop clerk to the most revered soldier in the Union.

As the returning hero of the Civil War, it was no surprise that he was viewed as a presidential candidate. Grant knew nothing of law or even the Constitution and had no interest in learning about them. However, Republican candidate Grant received the nomination of his party and won the presidential election of 1868 over Democrat Horatio Seymour.

Coming into office in 1869, 46-year-old President Grant chose people he thought he could trust and to whom he could delegate responsibility. Grant was loyal to a fault to those who worked with him. As a result, he was unwilling to remove dishonest or ineffective people. Therefore, the Grant administration was also routinely labeled one of the most corrupt in U. S. history. Despite this, Grant was re-elected to a second term in office.

Grant fought for the ratification of the Fifteenth Amendment, granting citizens the right to vote regardless of race or previous servitude, which angered many Southerners in the process. He sent in the military to protect African-Americans from newly formed terrorist groups such as the Ku Klux Klan.

Grant left the White House in 1877, admitting in his farewell address to Congress that it had been his "misfortune to be called to the Office of Chief Executive without any political training" and apologizing for his "errors of judgment."

Grant was then struck by financial disaster. Having invested most of his assets with his son's company, the son's partner lost it all. The former president was broke and relied on his friends to provide for him and his family.

To make money for his family, Grant agreed to write articles about the Civil War for *Century Magazine*. He then decided to write his memoirs when he found out he had throat cancer. The last days of his life were spent with Grant wrapped in blankets and in excruciating pain, slowly scrawling out his life's story. He completed the book just days before his death on July 23, 1885. Mark Twain had the memoirs published in book form, which ended up providing more than $500,000 to the Grant family. Grant's last campaign was a victorious one.

Rutherford B. Hayes

A broad-shouldered and handsome figure with a full beard, Rutherford B. Hayes was a cheerful, outgoing man whose love of people made him perfectly suited for public office.

Rutherford "Rud" Birchard Hayes was born on the evening of October 4, 1822, in the family home in Delaware, OH. He was delivered by Dr. Reuben Lamb for a fee of only $3.50. Unfortunately, Rutherford's father had died just 11 weeks before his birth. Already grieving the loss of a daughter and husband, Rud's mother, Sophia Birchard Hayes, was faced with the support of her two other children and a third one on the way. By renting out a farm for a portion of the crops and fruit it yielded, she was able to care for her children, especially Rud, who was a very sickly infant. When Rud was only two, his nine-year-old brother drown while ice skating.

Having never known his father, Rud was raised by his mother and bachelor uncle, Sardis Birchard. Sardi was very instrumental in serving as a surrogate father and providing the financial support for Sophia and her two children, as well as providing good educations for both Rud and his older sister, Fanny. Rud developed an unusually close bond with Fanny, who encouraged him to achieve the prominent career denied to her because she was a woman. He once referred to Fanny as "the confidante of all my life."

For a short time, Rud and Fanny attended a new publically supported district school. Rud later recalled, ". . . Schoolmaster, Daniel Granger . . . flogged great strapping fellows twice his size, throwing them through the walls of the school house. He once threw a large jack-knife . . . at the head of a boy who was whispering near me."

Rud attended Norwalk Seminary and, at 16, enrolled at Kenyon College where he took a special interest in philosophy and debate but detested science. He graduated class valedictorian in 1842.

After studying law for ten "vexatious and tedious" months in the law office of Thomas Sparrow, he entered Harvard Law School in 1843 and graduated in January 1845. He was admitted to the Ohio bar two months later. He then opened a practice in Uncle Sardi's town of Lower Sandusky. Bored and restless, Rutherford sought out a fresh start and moved to Cincinnati in 1849. In time, he made a name for himself in criminal law, defending society's

Artist Concept:

Hayes took a brisk walk daily down the streets of Washington, D. C., without the secret service! He was a collector of homemade canes and always carried one with him. The artist wanted to show him as a vigorous pedestrian striding down the streets of Rapid City.

Sculptor: Lee Leuning | Benefactors: The London Family: David, Cynthia, Amanda and Lily

81

outcasts. He often managed to free them or save them from the gallows.

Hayes vowed to marry by age 25. "Uppermost in the medley of ideas that are rolling about under my hair," he wrote at age 24, "is that before a year rolls around, I'll get me a wifey, or at least a sweetheart, if I can find one who agrees with me that I am one of the sunniest fellows in the world."

In 1847, Rutherford met Lucy Ware Webb, the daughter of a physician. (Much like Rutherford's own life experience, her father had died when she was an infant.) Lucy was not yet 16, and, as he later remembered, "not quite old enough to fall in love with." She enrolled at Wesleyan Woman's College and graduated in 1850. (She would be the first first lady to have graduated from college.) Thirty-year-old Rutherford married Lucy on December 30, 1852. The couple raised eight children, three of whom died. They began and ended every day with family prayer.

In July 1856, Hayes's beloved sister, Fanny, died from complications following the birth of twins. Fanny's death hit Hayes hard, but Lucy and their "fine little boys," as well as his newly kindled interest in politics, eased his grief.

A vigorous opponent of slavery, Mrs. Hayes contributed to her husband's decision to join the anti-slavery Republican Party. Hayes supported the Republican candidate for president who stood "for free states and against new slave states." When the lower Southern states seceded from the Union following President Abraham Lincoln's election in 1860, Hayes was willing to accept these actions but was outraged by South Carolina's attack on Fort Sumter. Having no military experience, he joined a volunteer company called the Burnet Rifles at the age of 40 with three sons and a fourth child on the way. He realized the nation was facing a long, hard struggle and declared, "I would prefer to go into it if I knew I was to die . . . than to live through and after it, without taking any part in it." On June 7, the governor of Ohio promoted Hayes to major in the 23rd Ohio Volunteers.

Hayes soon earned the respect of the enlisted men and his superiors. William McKinley, another future president and member of the 23rd Ohio Volunteers, marveled that "His whole nature seemed to change in battle from the sunny, agreeable, kind, generous, gentle gentleman he was. Once the battle was on . . . intense and ferocious."

At the 1862 Battle of South Mountain, Hayes spearheaded the attack on the rebels in Fox's Gap. When Hayes ordered a charge, a musket ball fractured his left arm above the elbow, leaving a gaping hole. Hayes survived, thanks to the skill of his brother-in-law, Dr. Joseph Webb, the regimental surgeon.

In July of 1864, Ohio Republicans nominated Hayes for a seat in the House of Representatives and suggested he come home and campaign. Hayes refused to leave the ferocious fighting, noting that "an officer fit for duty who, at this crisis, would abandon his post to electioneer for a seat in Congress ought to be scalped. You may feel perfectly sure I shall do no such thing." However, his last battle was on the horizon. On October 19, 1864, at Cedar Creek, Hayes's horse was shot out from under him. He was then hit in the head by a spent ball. His men assumed he had been killed, and his death was reported in the press. Wounded five times in the war, he was promoted to brigadier general "for gallant and distinguished services" and mustered out of the army in 1865. His statement refusing to leave the battle front was more effective politically than any stump speeches he could have made at home, and Hayes was elected to Congress in 1865.

In 1867, Hayes resigned from Congress and successfully ran for governor of Ohio for two terms. In 1874, Uncle Sardis died, leaving Hayes the bulk of his estate.

By 1876, Republicans recognized that Hayes, a war hero and a candidate acceptable to the Republican Party, was presidential material. Hayes received his party nomination, but he faced a tough campaign. Democratic opponent Samuel Tilden of New York was a superb political organizer. On election day, Tilden won the popular vote by 250,000 more votes than Hayes, but the vote in three Southern states was close enough for both parties to claim them. The one who won those states won the presidency. Congress set up a special commission to decide who carried those states, and the Republican majority commission awarded the disputed Electoral College votes to Hayes, making him the winner. Outraged and frustrated Democrats dubbed Hayes "Rutherfraud" and "His Fraudulency."

Once in office, however, Hayes proved to be scrupulously honest. His integrity and independence made him very popular with the general public. The death of Abraham Lincoln, the impeachment of Andrew Johnson and the failures of Ulysses S. Grant had left the presidency in a weakened state. Hayes helped to restore prestige to the office and heal the wounds left by the Civil War. He laid the foundation for the construction of the Panama Canal, vowing that any canal built in that region would be constructed and controlled by the U. S.

As first lady, Lucy brought her commitment to the temperance movement to the White House, banning all alcoholic beverages at state functions. Although rumor has it that the president sometimes ordered a special "dessert" laced with rum for a favored few without her knowledge, Lucy's strong stand against alcohol earned her the nickname, "Lemonade Lucy." Personally warm and kind, Lucy began the tradition of the Easter egg roll on the White House lawn. In addition, the telephone, typewriter and a permanent running water system made their appearance during their White House years.

Having renounced a second term four years earlier, Hayes retired happily to Spiegel Grove, the estate he had inherited from his uncle. Remaining active in public affairs, he encouraged temperance, opposed women's suffrage, promoted black education and advocated greater emphasis on prison reform. Lucy died from a stroke and was buried at Spiegel Grove on June 25, 1889.

In January 1893, Hayes caught cold from sitting in a drafty train car on his way home from Columbus. He went on to suffer a heart attack but rallied over the next couple of days until his heart suddenly gave out on January 17, 1893. His last words were, "I know that I am going where Lucy is."

James Garfield

James A. Garfield was born on a frontier farm in Cuyahoga County, OH, on November 19, 1831. He was the youngest of five children born to Abram and Eliza Ballou Garfield. Abram died when James was just an infant, so young James never got to know his father. James spent most of his childhood and early adolescence working in the fields of the family farm to help his widowed, near-penniless mother. James, like his father, loved the outdoors and a good fist fight, but he never liked the life of a farmer. A precocious child, he walked at nine months, climbed ladders at 10 months and was reading the Bible by the age of three. Garfield was perhaps the poorest man ever to become president and the only preacher to hold the highest office in this land.

White House Historical Association

Although very accident prone, James always had the dream of being a sailor. At the age of 17, he decided he would follow his dream and run away from home to work on the canal boats that shuttled between Pittsburg and Cleveland. Within the first six weeks, he fell overboard 14 times. The last time he fell, he became very ill with such a bad fever that he was sent home. While recovering, James realized that the way to his future success would have to be through brains and not brawn.

Determined to better his lot in life, he knew that a good education would be critical. In 1849, his mother gave him $17 to enter Geauga Seminary. He financed his schooling by working as a part-time carpenter and teacher. He proved he was up to the task of controlling a classroom by thrashing the local bully who drove out the previous schoolteacher.

At the age of 18, James underwent a religious conversion and was baptized into the Disciples of Christ and became a devout preacher in his church. From 1851 to 1854, he attended Eclectic Institute in Hiram, OH, which was a school founded by the Disciples of Christ. He earned a living as the school janitor. Some of his fellow students made him aware of how limited his life experiences were due to his religious background. He heard a piano played for the first time at 19, and he ate his first banana at the age of 23. Also at 23, James

Artist Concept:

Garfield has the sad distinction of being assassinated in office. He was born in a log cabin but shows no evidence of his humble beginnings in this presentation.

Sculptor: John Lopez | Benefactors: Nancy Todd Engler, Don and Joan Perdue

entered Williams College as one of the oldest students enrolled in the college.

James thrived academically at Williams and was a very serious student. However, he enjoyed hunting, fishing, billiards and drank (in moderation), despite the temperance movement at that time. He actively sought the company of ladies, once dating three young women at the same time. James was affectionate and often threw his arm around someone while speaking to them. This belied the fact that he had nightmares and severe headaches about his fragile self-confidence.

Eventually, James became enamored with Lucretia "Crete" Rudolph, who was one of his classmates at Eclectic Institute and a member of the Disciples of Christ. Lucretia was a very attractive young lady with a sharp intellect that equaled James's pursuit of knowledge. To help James finish his studies at Williams, Lucretia taught school. In 1856 after graduating with honors, James returned to Eclectic Institute to teach courses in classical languages, English, history, geology and mathematics. To entertain guests, Garfield was known to write Greek with one hand and Latin with the other.

James and Lucretia were married on November 11, 1858. He studied the law on his own, passing the Ohio bar exam in 1861. By then, Garfield was active in state politics, becoming the youngest member of the Ohio legislature. He was an enthusiastic abolitionist. When the Civil War broke out, Garfield and his fellow Eclectic Institute students joined the Union army. At the Battle of Chickamauga, even though his horse was shot out from under him, he safely delivered a dispatch that saved the army of Cumberland from disaster. For his bravery, he was given a battlefield promotion to major general—the youngest Union officer to ever achieve that rank. Garfield left the army in 1863.

He went on to serve in the U. S. Congress with distinction for the next 17 years. A powerful speaker and outspoken opponent of slavery during his term in Congress, Garfield was prepared for the presidency and hoped to make the office stronger than it had been since Lincoln's assassination. President Rutherford B. Hayes wrote in his diary of Garfield: "Truth is no man ever started so low that accomplished so much in all our history. Not Franklin or Lincoln even. . . He is the ideal candidate because he is the ideal self-made man." Running against fellow Civil War veteran, Wilford Scott Hancock, Garfield was elected president by less than one percent of the popular vote and was inaugurated on March 4, 1881.

Garfield's mother, Eliza, was the first mother of a president to attend her son's inauguration. She lived at the White House during his brief term in office. Being a frail woman and always dressing in black, it was customary for her son (who stood over six feet in height) to personally carry his mother up and down the White House stairs.

With a strong religious background, both James and Lucretia were able to live their lives and raise their five children in the surroundings of a loving family. They had a very deep, mutual love which allowed their marriage to survive marital discord over Garfield's brief affair with a woman from New York in 1862.

On July 2, 1881, Garfield was walking through Washington's Baltimore and Potomac train station, preparing to leave for Williams College to introduce his two sons to his alma mater. Shots rang out from a .44 British Bulldog, and Garfield was shot in the back by Charles Guiteau, a deranged man who resented the fact that the president had refused to appoint him to a European consulship. Guiteau chose the weapon specifically because he thought it would look impressive in a museum.

Garfield lived and continued to conduct the business of the presidency from his bed while in agonizing pain. Lucretia, although gravely ill with malaria and exhaustion herself, continued to care for the president during his struggle for life. The doctors, using dirty tools and unwashed hands, continued to search for the bullet, traumatizing Garfield's body until it caused a fatal heart attack. On September 19, 1881, at the age of 50 and serving as president for only 200 days, Garfield died with Lucretia at his side. An autopsy revealed that the bullet had been lodged in a protective cyst. It is believed that the president would have survived if the doctors had just left him alone.

Upon Garfield's death, Guiteau wrote to the new president of the United States, Chester A. Arthur, "My inspiration is a Godsend to you and I presume that you appreciate it . . . Never think of Garfield's removal as murder. It was an act of God, resulting from a political necessity for which he was responsible." Being found guilty at his trial, Guiteau was sentenced to be hanged. At his death, he was still convinced that he had done God's work.

Murdered within months of his inauguration, Garfield served too briefly to have left much of a legacy. Many decisions he made lacked judgment, and he was too dependent on those around him. His leadership was basically untested, and the times did not demand a president of heroic standing. Therefore, Garfield could be remembered as a martyr above all else—as one who truly gave his life for his nation.

An engraving of James A. Garfield's assassination, published in *Frank Leslie's Illustrated Newspaper.*

Chester Arthur

Known as "The Gentleman Boss" of the Republican Party in New York and a behind-the-scenes politician, Chester A. Arthur never won an election to public office on his own.

Born to Malvina Arthur and Reverend William Arthur (a Baptist minister and passionate abolitionist), Chester was born on October 5, 1829, in a small log cabin in Fairfield, VT. The fifth of eight children, Chester and his family moved seven times from one Baptist parish to another throughout Vermont and New York. His fundamental education of reading and writing came from home.

Portrait by Peter Hansen Balling

Even as a young lad, Chester was known to be organized. "You might see him in the village street after a shower, watching boys building a mud dam," a classmate recalled. "Pretty soon he would be ordering this one to bring stones, another sticks, and others sod and mud to finish the dam."

Young Chet attended schools in New York where his father preached. At 15, he entered Union College in Schenectady, NY, and joined the college social fraternity. He was an average student who was more interested in living the good life than studying. Known for playing pranks with his fellow students, he once dumped the school bell into the Erie Canal.

Admitted to Phi Beta Kappa in his senior year, he graduated in the top third of the class of 1848, at the age of 18. Arthur was very clear about what he wanted to do with his life. His plans were to reside in Manhattan as a wealthy lawyer and public servant, living the life of a true gentleman.

After studying the law and teaching school, he became a student in the law office of Erastus D. Culver in 1853, and the next year, he was admitted to the bar to practice law in his own right as a member of Culver's firm.

An ardent abolitionist, Arthur took on a much publicized case in 1855 when he represented Lizzie Jennings, a black woman who was thrown off a New York City horse-car because of her color. Arthur won $225 in damages from the transit company and $25 from

Artist Concept:

Arthur is depicted as dignified and handsome with a clean-shaven chin and side whiskers, giving his presidential oath in a presidential manner.

Sculptor: John Lopez | Benefactor: Anonymous donor from Nebraska

the court. This case forced all New York City railroad companies to seat black passengers without prejudice on their streetcars. This lawsuit was brought 100 years before African-American Rosa Parks spurred a city-wide boycott for refusing to give up her seat to a white woman on a bus. As a result, the city of Montgomery, AL, lifted the law requiring segregation on public buses in 1955.

In 1859, 29-year-old Arthur met Ellen Lewis Herndon, the 22-year-old daughter of a U. S. Navy officer. Chester and "Nell" married on October 25, 1859. They had three children, although the eldest boy died in infancy. They were married for 20 years until Mrs. Arthur died from pneumonia the year before her husband became president. The marriage was nearing a separation at the time of her death, as she was becoming intolerant of his aloofness, his late hours and his love of feasting with his cronies. However, Arthur was deeply affected by her death and had fresh flowers put next to her portrait in the White House every day of his presidency.

Always working behind the scenes in the political arena, Arthur worked hard to get Republican Governor Edwin D. Morgan re-elected in 1860. When the Civil War broke out, Morgan rewarded Arthur by appointing him as acting quartermaster general to help equip over 200,000 volunteer troops. The next year, the governor promoted Arthur to state inspector general of militia with the rank of brigadier general. His lifelong talent for organizing made him very successful in this position. Arthur hoped to serve in a battlefield position, but Ellen, a Virginian with family members serving in the Confederacy, could not tolerate the thought of her husband taking up arms against them. Arthur respected his wife's wishes and remained in the quartermaster's office.

Arthur then turned his efforts toward General Ulysses S. Grant's nomination and election to the presidency in 1868. Grant appointed Arthur as collector of the Port of New York, which was the most important federal job in that city, controlling the appointment of more than 1,300 employees of the Custom House. Although there is no evidence of corruption on Arthur's part, he routinely supplemented his income by sharing a portion of all fines on imports. In his first year, his "perks" raised his original salary of $12,000 to $50,000 a year—a salary equivalent to the president of the United States at that time.

When Grant left office, newly elected President Rutherford B. Hayes set up a special panel to investigate scandals within the customs office. The panel found political favoritism and corruption in giving appointments and exposed the blatant practice of salary kickbacks. Hayes fired Arthur from his position, and Arthur returned to his law practice, continuing to use the title "General" the rest of his life.

In 1880, Arthur was nominated to be James Garfield's vice-presidential candidate. The Garfield-Arthur ticket went on to win the national election by a very narrow margin. Upon the assassination attempt on Garfield just 200 days into his presidency, Arthur took the oath of office as president of the United States on September 20, 1881, at his home in New York City.

Because of earlier dealings within the Custom House and other questionable transactions in his early political life, the nation was shocked when Arthur was elevated to the presidency. The word "politician" had become synonymous with "corrupt." Hayes had made Arthur the very symbol of evil after dismissing him from the collector of the Port of New York position. Even a leading Republican said, "Chet Arthur President of the United States! Good God!"

But the country was pleasantly surprised when Arthur turned out to be an honest, conscientious leader. He decried his reputation as a slick politician who put his own party loyalty over the needs of the nation at large. He began American participation in international, political, cultural and scientific conferences. He called a meeting of all the countries of the Western Hemisphere to find ways to prevent war. Arthur supported the Pendleton Act of 1883 to counter cronyism by requiring competitive exams for government employment, banning salary kickbacks. This process ensured that hiring and promotions were based on merit not connections.

When President Arthur first entered the White House, the wealthy new president felt it was too shabby for his tastes. For the first three months of his presidency, he lived elsewhere while redecoration was being done. Always the flamboyant, stylish gentleman, Arthur employed New York designer Louis Tiffany to completely renovate the White House. He also installed an elevator for his convenience. Arthur had a reputation of being a distant, uninvolved father to his two children, but he loved to showcase them at White House social affairs. He preferred fishing, living the bachelor life and administrative work to family life. He also harbored a secret. Diagnosed in 1882 with Bright's disease (a fatal kidney disease) he knew he would not be able to run for a second term. Arthur was once quoted as saying, "I may be president of the United States, but my private life is nobody's damned business."

In 1884, Arthur returned to the practice of law after leaving the presidency, but his failing health kept him from doing too much. On November 18, 1886, only two years after leaving office, Arthur died at home with his children and sister at his side at the age of 56. At his funeral, pallbearers included Robert T. Lincoln, General Philip H. Sheridan, Charles L. Tiffany and Cornelius Vanderbilt. He was buried next to his wife in the Arthur family plot.

Publisher Alexander K. McClure described Arthur this way: "No man ever entered the presidency so profoundly and widely distrusted, and no one ever retired . . . more generally respected."

Twenty-second & Twenty-fourth President of the United States of America

Grover Cleveland

President Grover Cleveland was the first Democrat elected after the Civil War. He was also the only president to leave the White House and return for a second term four years later.

Stephen Grover Cleveland was born on March 18, 1837, in Caldwell, NJ, the fifth of nine children. His father, Reverend Richard Falley Cleveland, was an ordained Presbyterian minister, and his mother, Ann Neal, was the daughter of a wealthy law book publisher. Grover was four years old when the family moved to Fayetteville, NY. They then moved 10 years later to Clinton, NY.

Library of Congress

A fun-loving, responsible child, Grover took time out of his chores to fish in Green Lake or swim in Limestone Creek. He also learned the value of using his time wisely. For example, nine-year-old Grover wrote an essay, which read, "If we expect to become great and good men, and be respected and esteemed by our friends, we must improve our time when we are young."

At 15, Grover left his family in Clinton to work as a store clerk in Fayetteville for $50 a year plus room and board. It was his hope to go to college, but his father's death in 1853 ended any hopes for his further education. Cleveland had to go to work to help support his mother and eight siblings.

Cleveland did not fight in the Civil War. At that time, it was legal to buy a substitute. Therefore, Cleveland paid at least $150 to have someone else go to battle in his place. Later in his political career, this fact was used against him, but Cleveland argued that it was necessary so he could stay home and care for his mother and younger siblings.

Later while visiting his uncle, Lewis F. Allen, in Buffalo, he was persuaded to settle there. His uncle was a successful stock breeder, and Grover was offered $10 a month plus room and board to edit *The American Shorthorn Handbook*. Allen also arranged for him to study law at a local law office, and Cleveland was admitted to the bar in 1859.

He then practiced law with the firm of Rogers, Bowen and Rogers and became

Artist Concept:

Since Cleveland's refuge was his library, the sculptor portrayed him with one of his books. His seriousness and integrity were traits the sculptor tried to capture in the president's expression seen here.

Sculptor: James Maher | Benefactors: Arthur and Sarah Ludwick

associated with the Democratic Party. After experiencing a victory as assistant district attorney for Erie County and a loss as district attorney, he returned to practice law with Oscar Folsom in 1865.

In 1871, Cleveland began seeing Mrs. Maria Halpin, a 33-year-old widow from Buffalo, who kept company with various men. In September 1874, she gave birth to a son and named Cleveland as the father. Although Cleveland was unsure of the child's paternity, he agreed to pay child support but chose not to marry her. Later, this story came up during his presidential campaign. When asked by his party what to do, he simply said, "Tell the truth." His direct honesty calmed the issue, but the campaign chant against him continued: "Ma, Ma, where's my Pa? Gone to the White House, Ha, Ha, Ha!"

In 1871, Cleveland was voted sheriff of Eric County, NY. He earned a reputation for fearlessness and incorruptibility, which he retained throughout his career. While serving as sheriff, he was called upon twice to execute convicted prisoners. Not wanting to pass this responsibility on to anyone else, Cleveland sprang the trapdoor himself. After his term as sheriff, he returned again to his private law practice.

In 1882, Cleveland was elected mayor of Buffalo, NY. He became known as the "veto mayor" for his repeated efforts to end graft and overpriced contracts. He was known for his no-nonsense "ugly-honest" approach, earning himself the nickname, "His Obstinacy." His honest, efficient administration at City Hall prompted the newspapers to support Cleveland for governor in June 1882, and he easily won the race in 1883.

As governor, he vetoed several private bills and treasury grabs. He insisted that merit, not party service, be the sole criteria for governmental appointments. He instilled closer scrutiny of state banking practices. Cleveland was immediately considered by Democrats as presidential material.

At the Democratic National Convention in Chicago in July 1884, Cleveland was the clear front-runner. In his nomination speech, Edward Bragg of Wisconsin roused the delegates with a slap at Tammany Hall, a strong New York political-machine opposing Cleveland. "They love him, gentleman," Bragg said of Cleveland, "and they respect him, not only for himself, for his character, for his integrity and judgment, and iron will, but they love him most of all for the enemies he has made." Cleveland won the nomination and was elected in 1884. With a sparse political background and only modest success as a lawyer, this Buffalo attorney launched perhaps the most spectacular rise in American politics at that time.

A 47-year-old bachelor, Cleveland was hardworking, conscientious and methodical. On the other hand, he could be very stubborn. Reporters didn't know what to think of him. One journalist remarked of the 260-pound president: "He just eats and works."

Cleveland was ill at ease at first with all the comforts the White House offered him. "I must go to dinner," he wrote a friend, "but I wish it was to eat pickled herring, Swiss cheese and a chop at Louis' (Cleveland's favorite restaurant) instead of the French stuff I shall find."

While working in the White House, Cleveland had an enormous workload. Rather than trust his subordinates, Cleveland chose to micromanage their work or do it himself. He sometimes worked until two or three o'clock in the morning. During his first term, Cleveland even answered the White House telephone himself. He actually scheduled his wedding for 7:00 p.m. in the evening so he could work a full day.

Two years into his first term, Cleveland, 49, quietly married Frances Folsom, 21, on June 2, 1886, in the Blue Room of the White House. This was the only presidential marriage performed in the White House itself. The wedding ceremony was small and simple with the music provided by John Philip Sousa and the Marine Band.

The bride was the daughter of Oscar Folsom, Cleveland's former law partner. Cleveland, at 27, met his future wife just after she was born, buying her a baby carriage and doting on her as she grew up. When her father died in 1875 without a will, Cleveland was appointed administrator of his estate and advocate for 11-year-old Frances's welfare. Sometime while Frances was in college, Cleveland's feelings for her took a romantic turn, and he proposed in August 1885 soon after her graduation.

Frances was a tall, pretty girl with dark hair and dark eyes with an excellent sense of humor that she wasn't afraid to use in public. When Cleveland became president, she became the youngest first lady in history. Upon leaving the White House after Cleveland's first term, Frances told the staff, "Keep the furniture, we'll be back." The couple had five children. Their first born, Ruth, had the candy bar, "Baby Ruth," named after her. Another daughter, Esther, was the first baby born in the White House.

Defeated by Benjamin Harrison in his bid for re-election, Cleveland returned to his law practice until he was elected for a second term in 1892.

In 1893, Cleveland complained about a rough spot on the roof of his mouth, and doctors found it to be cancerous. Cleveland chose to have the surgery kept secret. On June 30, 1893, he boarded a friend's yacht anchored on the East River in New York, and the next morning, the doctors removed the cancerous tissue and the upper part of his jaw. An artificial jaw made of rubber preserved his jowly expression, and no one ever detected the surgery. The public was not told about the operation, since Cleveland believed news of his illness might lead to a panic on Wall Street. In fact, the operation wasn't made public until after Cleveland's death.

When the Pullman Strike of 1894 shut down mail trains running in and out of Chicago, Cleveland sent in federal troops to quell the violence. "If it takes the entire army and navy of the U.S. to deliver a post card in Chicago," he thundered, "that card will be delivered." Samuel Tilden once said of Cleveland, "Backbone! He has so much of it, it makes him stick out in front!" Cleveland vetoed many private pensions to Civil War veterans whose claims were found to be fraudulent. When Congress passed a bill granting pensions for veterans with non-military disabilities, he vetoed that, too. During his two terms as president, Cleveland issued more vetoes than all previous presidents combined.

On June 24, 1908, after years of suffering from rheumatism and kidney disease, his health steadily declined, and Cleveland died of heart failure. His last words were, "I have tried so hard to do right."

Benjamin Harrison

The family name of "Harrison" was prominent throughout the early years of this country's history—from the signing of the Declaration of Independence in 1776 to the presidency of the United States in 1889. President Benjamin Harrison was named after his great-grandfather, Colonel Benjamin Harrison, a signer of the Declaration of Independence and governor of Virginia. His paternal grandfather, William Henry Harrison, was the ninth president of the U. S. in 1841.

Library of Congress

Young Benjamin was born on August 20, 1833, in North Bend, OH, at the home of his presidential grandfather. Ben was one of nine children born to John Scott Harrison, a prosperous farmer and congressman, and Elizabeth Irwin Harrison, John's second wife. She was a devout Presbyterian and a strict, unaffectionate mother. Elizabeth died in childbirth a few days before Benjamin's 17th birthday.

Born into a family with a legacy of political involvement, Benjamin believed he was destined for important work. This confidence was sometimes perceived as arrogance. He developed a stiff and formal personality, later being referred to as "the human iceberg."

Living in a rural area, John Harrison built a log one-room schoolhouse and hired a teacher to educate his children in reading, writing and arithmetic. Ben's first teacher, Harriet Root, pronounced him "the brightest of the family . . . determined to go ahead in everything, but," she added, ". . . terribly stubborn about many things."

Benjamin hunted, fished, hauled wood and tended livestock on his father's 600-acre farm. He thoroughly enjoyed country life, free from what he considered the foul, unwholesome air of Cincinnati. At a young age, Ben came up with this insight: "The manner by which women are treated is a good criterion to judge of the true state of society. . . . for as society advances, the true character of woman is discovered."

At the age of 14, Ben attended Farmers' College, a preparatory school in Cincinnati, where he developed a lifelong interest in history, politics and sociology. During these college

Artist Concept:

Since Harrison was not very sociable and his handlers tried to limit his contact with the public, the artist portrayed him as being alone in his garden feeding the birds, which gave him respite from the stress of being president.

Sculptor: John Lopez | Benefactor: The Beck Family

years, 14-year-old Benjamin met 15-year-old Caroline Lavinia Scott, daughter of Reverend Scott, who was a professor of chemistry and physics.

Two years later, he transferred to Miami University in Oxford, OH, where he took a particular interest in debate. He also rekindled his friendship with Caroline, who was attending the Oxford Female Institute. He became an outstanding public speaker. For the next two years, he constantly courted "Carrie," and they became secretly engaged. Harrison graduated in 1852, ranking fourth in his class of 16 boys.

Throughout his early life, his ambitions were torn between the ministry and the law. After graduation, he decided to become a lawyer rather than a minister, and he studied at the Cincinnati law office of Storer and Gwynne from 1852 until he was admitted to the bar in 1854. On October 20, 1853, 20-year-old Harrison married Carrie, his college sweetheart. The ceremony was small and simple and was officiated by Carrie's father, Reverend Scott. The newlyweds moved to Indianapolis, IN, where they lived in a boardinghouse while Ben worked as crier of the federal court at a salary of $2.50 a day. This gave him the opportunity to become acquainted with most of the lawyers in town, and William Wallace invited young Benjamin to go into partnership with him the following year.

In 1856 he joined the new Republican Party and was soon elected the Indianapolis city attorney at a salary of $400 per year. In 1860, Harrison was elected to the office of reporter to the Supreme Court of Indiana.

In 1862, the Civil War was at its peak. Harrison was offered command of the 70th Indiana Infantry Regiment. He served for three years and was promoted to brigadier general. Serving under Major General William T. Sherman in the Atlanta campaign, Harrison was among the first of the Union forces to march into the city upon its surrender. Sherman stated that Harrison served with "foresight, discipline and a fighting spirit . . ." Even with such achievements and praise, Harrison thought war was a dirty business that no decent man would find pleasurable.

After the war, Harrison returned to his law practice and continued his active participation in state politics. After many unsuccessful campaigns for office, he was finally elected to the U. S. Senate from 1881 to 1887. In 1888, at the Republican National Convention, a deadlock prevented the party to elect its presidential nominee. On the eighth ballot, Harrison was elected (primarily because he was "safe" and would be easy to control). After an election in which Harrison received fewer popular votes than his opponent, President Grover Cleveland, the Electoral College gave Harrison the victory with 233 votes to Cleveland's 168.

History books portray Harrison as a lightweight puppet of political-party bosses. He was viewed as one who sleepwalked through the presidency. Among one of the best extemporaneous speakers of his day, Harrison could charm a crowd of 30,000 with powerful speeches but could make them all enemies with a single handshake. One visitor to the White House described his handshake as "grasping a wet petunia." Since he disliked small talk, he could not talk for two minutes in a room of five people. Harrison was known as

"Little Ben," not out of affection but because of his height. Only 5'6" tall with a potbelly perched on spindly legs, he resembled a medieval gnome.

Although lacking in charisma and the common touch, he was widely respected for his intelligence, honesty and attention to duty and diligence. Biographer Henry J. Sievers wrote, "Integrity formed the backbone of Harrison's character. His active intellect firmly backed by moral courage was regarded as a bulwark of political decency."

Although Harrison was stiff and formal with acquaintances, he opened up with his family. He spent as little time as possible in the office, working only until noon each day. When he and Caroline moved into the White House, so did their two children and grandchildren. He loved to play with his grandchildren, and they were allowed to keep as many pets on the grounds as they wanted, including a goat whom they named Old Whiskers. Harrison once chased the goat down Pennsylvania Avenue with his three grandchildren in tow, holding his top hat in one hand while waving his cane with the other. He was an avid duck hunter, billiards player and cigar smoker. One of his hunting trips made the national press when he shot a farmer's pig by mistake.

First Lady Caroline secured $35,000 from Congress to renovate the White House. She purged the mansion of its growing rodent and insect population, laid new floors, installed new plumbing and added more bathrooms. The White House also received new paint job and wallpaper. In 1891, she installed electricity, but she was so afraid of it that she refused to handle the switches. Instead, she left the lights on all night until the engineer came in to turn them off in the morning. In 1889, she put up the first White House Christmas tree. Mrs. Harrison also served as the first president-general of the Daughters of the American Revolution. Unfortunately, Caroline contracted tuberculosis and died just two weeks before election day for Harrison's second term.

After being defeated in his bid for a second presidential term, Harrison retired to his home in Indianapolis, although it was terribly difficult for the former president to contemplate life without his wife. Sometime after though, Harrison fell in love with Mary Scott Lord Dimmick, Caroline's widowed niece who had served as the first lady's assistant in the White House. On April 6, 1896, 62-year-old Harrison married 37-year-old Dimmick. Harrison's grown children from his first marriage were horrified at the news and refused to attend the wedding.

Harrison undertook a very active retirement, resuming his law practice and writing articles for national magazines. On March 13, 1901, at the age of 67, Harrison died in his home after a bout of the flu, which resulted in a fatal case of pneumonia.

Theodore Roosevelt once said, "Damn the President! He is a cold-blooded, narrow-minded, prejudiced, obstinate, timid old psalm-singing Indianapolis politician." In 1918, Henry Adams wrote, "Mr. Harrison was an excellent president, a man of ability and force; perhaps the best president the Republican Party had put forward since Lincoln's death. Harrison has been assigned to the rankings of mediocrity." He is remembered as an average president, who was not among the best but certainly not among the worst.

William McKinley

Historians once considered President William McKinley a mediocre president who had an indecisive nature that swayed with public opinion and the wishes of his political cronies. He was not viewed as taking firm stands on national and international issues. He was once described as "having his ear so close to the ground, it was full of grasshoppers."

Courtney Art Studio

Current opinions vastly differ. Bringing the nation into the 20th century, McKinley made moves that are now considered revolutionary to elevate the United States as a powerful empire on the world stage. For example, once considered weak during the Spanish-American crisis, he is now viewed as a president who tried mightily to avoid war. Theodore Roosevelt, then assistant secretary of the navy, called McKinley a "white-livered cur . . . having no more backbone than a chocolate éclair." Eventually, though, McKinley changed the make-up of America as a world power by declaring war on Spain on April 25, 1898, to secure independence for Cuba. By February 6, 1899, under the Paris Peace Treaty, Spain relinquished its claim to Cuba and ceded Puerto Rico, Guam and the Philippine Islands to the U. S. for $20 million. Practically overnight, the United States became an international, colonial power. He also negotiated the annexation of Hawaii and created an "open door" policy with China to create the link needed between foreign markets and national prosperity.

William was born on January 29, 1843, in the small town of Niles, OH. His parents, William McKinley, Sr., and Nancy Allison McKinley, raised eight children with the values and virtues that they personally embraced. The elder McKinley was a successful owner of an iron foundry and instilled in young William a strong work ethic and respectful attitude. His mother was devoutly religious, teaching him the value of prayer, courtesy and honesty in all dealings. William recounted his childhood as fun-filled, including swimming, hunting, fishing, ice skating, camping and horseback riding. During the Mexican War, he and his playmates had great fun drilling like soldiers.

Artist Concept:

McKinley was the first president to use the telephone to campaign. Also, the president traditionally wore a fresh red carnation in his lapel every day. Since he was assassinated while stopping to give his good luck carnation away to a child, he is shown with a red carnation in his lapel.

Sculptor: Lee Leuning | Benefactors: Arthur and Sarah Ludwick

Education was a priority for William. He learned the fundamentals at a public school. When the family moved to Poland, OH, he finished his elementary school education and enrolled at the Methodist Poland Seminary. It had always been his mother's dream that William would become a Methodist minister, but his studies introduced him to public speaking. A naturally gifted speaker, he organized and served as president of the school's Everett Literary and Debating Society.

After graduating from seminary, 17-year-old William entered Allegheny College at Meadville, PA, but a downturn in family finances and illness forced William back home within a year. He taught school for one year in 1860 and clerked in the town post office until Civil War broke out and William joined the 23rd Ohio Volunteer Infantry in June 1861 at the age of 18.

Entering as a private, he proved himself a valiant soldier on the battlefield. At the Battle of Antietam, he demonstrated marked valor in transporting much-needed rations to troops at the front under fire. At Winchester, VA, in July 1864, he carried orders to the front and risked his life to retrieve heavy artillery. The day after this engagement, he was promoted to captain. His commander, Rutherford B. Hayes, a future president of the U. S., promoted McKinley to brevet major, saying, "Young as he was, we soon found that in the business of a soldier, requiring much executive ability, young McKinley showed unusual and unsurpassed capacity, especially for a boy of his age. When battles were fought or service was to be performed in warlike things, he always filled his place." McKinley ended his four-year stint in the military but retained his relationship with Hayes, whom he considered his mentor throughout the rest of his life.

When the Civil War ended, McKinley returned to Ohio to begin his career in law and politics. He studied law at a Youngstown office of Judge Glidden. He briefly attended Albany Law School but dropped out before graduation. He was admitted to the Ohio bar in March 1867. While practicing law in Canton, he became involved with the Republican Party. He was elected county prosecutor in 1869 and then ran successfully for Congress in 1877. McKinley returned to Ohio to run for governor in 1891, which he won by the narrowest of margins. By 1896, with strong support from the Republican Party and private support from industry, McKinley was swept into the presidency by one of the largest margins of victory in history.

In 1867, William met the beautiful and charming Ida Saxton, daughter of a prominent Canton banker. She was a graduate of Brook Hall Seminary, which was a finishing school in Pennsylvania. McKinley began actively courting Ida upon her return from a European tour in 1869. William, 27, married Ida, 23, on January 25, 1871. Although this marriage began under the best of circumstances, it soon took its toll on the couple. Over a short span of time, Ida's two daughters died in infancy and her mother died. As a result of this physical and emotional trauma, Ida developed epilepsy and semi-infantile behavior, became dependant on drugs and was totally dependent on her husband for the rest of his life.

By all accounts, McKinley was open, friendly, even-tempered, cheerful, optimistic and universally well-liked. "McKinley was more than popular," according to historian Margaret

Leech. "He was beloved . . . Even his political opponents were attracted by the peculiar sweetness of his personality," Another biographer concluded, "His uniform courtesy and fairness commanded the admiration of Democrats as well as Republicans . . . The general public found him free from vanity or affectation." Yet, he did not gush with emotion. Rather, he worked a subtle charm effective with people from all walks of life. Although not a particularly gifted storyteller, he enjoyed a good clean joke but bristled at off-color remarks.

With this type of demeanor, there was no question that William would extend every kindness and concern for his invalid wife. It was said that he never left her side for more than an hour. During his political campaign, McKinley chose to stand on his front porch and give brief talks to the delegates or use the telephone as a campaign tool. He broke with presidential tradition by seating his wife next to him at all state dinners so that he could quickly put a handkerchief or napkin over her face to hide her facial contortions if an epileptic attack occurred. He would leave any meeting or occasion to rush to her side when she called, even if it was only to ask for a glass of water or a writing pen. The president's patient devotion and loving attention was the talk of the capital. Political advisor Mark Hanna remarked, "President McKinley has made it pretty hard for the rest of us husbands here in Washington."

McKinley always dressed conservatively and refused to be photographed unless he was impeccably groomed. During political campaigns, he wore a red carnation in his buttonhole for good luck. The president loved to circulate in large crowds of well-wishers, extending one-pump handshakes (once documented at 134 in a minute) to lines of the general public. It is that exact ritual which led to the end of McKinley's life.

On September 6, 1901, shortly after McKinley's second presidential inauguration, he visited the Pan American Exposition in Buffalo, NY. Despite warnings from the secret service, McKinley insisted on "pressing the flesh" at the Temple of Music on the exposition grounds. McKinley reached out to shake the bandaged hand of a man in line, only to hear two sharp cracks from a .32 Iver Johnson revolver delivered by Leon F. Czolgosz, a mentally unstable unemployed wire millworker.

When McKinley fell to the ground, he made two statements. Seeing his assailant being restrained, he cried out, "Don't let them hurt him!" He then whispered to his secretary, "My wife, be careful how you tell her—oh, be careful!" Despite all the efforts of the surgeons who attended McKinley, they were unable to locate the bullet. (One bullet hit McKinley's vest button and did not enter the skin). On September 14, 1901, McKinley died of apparent gangrene from the unattended wound at the age of 58. Aptly, President McKinley was once quoted as saying, "That's all a man can hope for during his lifetime—to set an example—and when he is dead, to be an inspiration for history."

Theodore Roosevelt

President Theodore Roosevelt craved the limelight. As one observer put it, Roosevelt set out to be "the bride at every wedding, the corpse at every funeral." He was fearless, decisive, ambitious, proud and irresistibly charming to men and women alike. He loved children and often took the time to romp with them or gather them for a story. He captivated listeners with tales of his adventures out West. He detested dirty jokes and typically walked away in the middle of a story as soon as he detected its off-color nature. Whether delivering speeches to large crowds or having private conversations, Roosevelt spoke forcefully, gesturing constantly and pounding his fist in the air to stress a point, while jerking to and fro with each word.

Theodore Roosevelt, Jr., was born on October 27, 1858, in New York City, the second of four children. His father, Theodore Roosevelt, Sr., was a wealthy businessman and philanthropist. His mother, Martha "Mittie" Roosevelt, was a southerner raised on a plantation in Georgia.

"Teedie" grew up with the love of his parents and siblings, but he was always a sickly child, as he suffered from asthma. At the age of 13, he was given a gun, but he could not hit the bull's eye. It was determined that he was nearsighted and needed glasses. About the same time, he was bullied by four other boys on a stagecoach ride, but he couldn't fight them because he was so sickly. Encouraged by the elder Roosevelt, he undertook a program of gymnastics and weight lifting in a gym built by his father on the second floor of their house. He developed a rugged physique and became an advocate of exercise and the "strenuous life." He always found time for physical activities, including hiking, riding horses and swimming. He even sometimes skinny-dipped in the icy waters of the Potomac River in the winter.

As a young boy, Theodore had private tutors. He traveled widely through Europe and the Middle East. When he entered Harvard College in 1876, he studied German, natural history, zoology, forensics and composition. He also tried wrestling and boxing but wasn't very good at it because he couldn't see his opponent without his glasses. His excellent grades won him election to Phi Beta Kappa, and he graduated magna cum laude in 1880.

Artist Concept:

This bronze statue features a young Roosevelt in his Rough Rider uniform. The blue polka-dot kerchief around his neck was a signature part of his uniform. Roosevelt was a robust president, and the sculptor artfully captures his larger-than-life personality.

Sculptor: John Lopez | Benefactors: Dale and Jacquolyn Fullerton

During college, Roosevelt fell in love with Alice Hathaway Lee, a young woman from a prominent New England banking family. They married on Theodore's 22nd birthday on October 27, 1880. Roosevelt took his bride on a tour of Europe in the summer of 1881 and climbed the Matterhorn in Switzerland during this trip. He launched his career in public service when he was elected to the New York assembly and served two terms from 1882 to 1884.

A double tragedy struck Roosevelt in 1884. On February 12, 1884, Alice gave birth to a daughter named Alice Lee. Two days later, Roosevelt's mother died of typhoid fever and his wife died of complications of birth and Bright's disease (a fatal kidney disease) on the same day in the same house. "When my heart's dearest died," Roosevelt wrote, "the light went from my life forever." For the next few months, a devastated Roosevelt threw himself into politics to escape his grief. Finally, he left his daughter in the care of his sister and fled to the Dakota Badlands (in present-day North Dakota).

Arriving out West, Roosevelt savored the frontier life. He bought two ranches and bought a thousand head of cattle. He flourished in the hardships of frontier life, riding for days, hunting grizzly bears, herding cows and chasing outlaws as a frontier sheriff. When most of his cattle were lost in the blizzards of 1886 and 1887, he returned to the East.

In October 1886, Roosevelt agreed to run for mayor of New York City as the Republican candidate. When he lost the election, everyone agreed that Roosevelt's political future looked black. The humor magazine, *Puck*, wrote, "You are not the timber of which presidents are made."

Another reason Roosevelt returned East was because of a rediscovered love with his childhood sweetheart, Edith Kermit Carow. Edith lived next door to the Roosevelts and was his first real playmate outside his family. As adolescents, their mutual love of books and nature evolved into romance, but after Theodore went away to Harvard and met Alice Lee, they drifted apart. The year after his wife's death, he ran into Miss Carow, and they began seeing each other. On December 2, 1886, 28-year-old Theodore married 25-year-old Edith in London, England. Theodore and Edith had six children, including Alice Lee.

After campaigning vigorously for President Benjamin Harrison, Roosevelt was rewarded by an appointment to the U. S. Civil Service Commission, serving for six years. Then, New York City Mayor William Strong appointed Roosevelt to commissioner of the corruption-ridden police force. He forced the resignation of the chief of police for fraud and kickbacks and adopted the practice of prowling streets at night in a black cape on the lookout for policemen not doing their duty. Newspapers reported his diligence to reform the city police. This made him very popular, until he insisted upon enforcing Sunday blue laws, which closed saloons. As a result, New Yorkers were glad to see him go when he was appointed assistant secretary of the navy under President William McKinley.

When the Spanish-American War began, Roosevelt resigned his position with the navy to volunteer for service as commander of the 1st U. S. Volunteer Cavalry, a unit known as the Rough Riders. It was an elite company of Ivy League polo players, cowboys, sheriffs, prospectors, police officers and Native Americans. On July 1, Roosevelt achieved glory when he led the Rough Riders in a charge up San Juan Hill on foot and in the face of intense enemy fire, losing a fourth of his men. He later wrote about his military exploits: "I would rather have led that charge and earned my colonelcy than served three terms in the U. S. Senate. . . . "

Certainly San Juan made his political career. Roosevelt immediately won the Republican nomination for governor of New York and won the election. After taking office in 1899, his office further alienated the Republican Party machine by forcing the legislature to pass a tax on corporate franchises. He once commented: "I have always been fond of the West African proverb: 'Speak softly and carry a big stick, you will go far.'"

By early 1900, the Republicans of New York wanted to get rid of this young governor that they could not control. They began talk of "pushing him upstairs" into the vice presidency. At the Republican National Convention, Roosevelt made the re-nominating speech for President McKinley. The convention went wild, nominating him as McKinley's running mate by acclamation. However Mark Hanna, the Republican national chairman, was not pleased. He warned, "Don't any of you realize that there's only one life between this madman and the White House?" In November, McKinley and Roosevelt were elected by a huge margin.

Roosevelt found the vice presidency very dull. To pass the time before Congress convened in December, he went on a hunting and fishing excursion. There he received word that McKinley had been seriously wounded by an assassination in New York. He rushed to McKinley's bedside but was assured that the president would recover, so he left to join his family in the Adirondacks. On September 13, 1901, during a mountain-climbing expedition, Roosevelt was informed that the president was dying. In the house where McKinley's body lay, 43-year-old Roosevelt was sworn in as the youngest president in history (at that time). In 1904, Roosevelt won a landslide victory for re-election.

As president, his "Square Deal" domestic program reformed the American workplace, initiating welfare laws and government regulation of industry. He was the nation's first president who was a conservationist, setting aside 200 million acres for national forests, reserves and wildlife preserves. He wanted to make the U. S. a global power, believing that the world should settle international disputes through diplomacy rather than war. For his role in negotiating a peace agreement between the Russians and Japan in 1906, Roosevelt became the first American to win the Nobel Peace Prize. He also initiated the building of the Panama Canal. For eight years, he used his popularity to win votes, to shape issues and to mold opinions. In the process, he changed the executive office forever in so many ways.

After retiring in 1909 at the age of 50, Roosevelt made an attempt to re-enter politics to no avail. In 1910, while campaigning, John Shrank tried to assassinate him. The bullet passed through the pages of his speech and a metal eyeglass case. Luckily, it only broke a rib and Roosevelt recovered completely. On January 6, 1919, Roosevelt died from a blood clot to his heart from recurrences of malaria and a leg infection he contracted during an earlier expedition to Brazil.

William Taft

William Howard Taft was a man of huge stature—6'2" tall and weighing in excess of 300 pounds—but was dominated for most of his life by two women. His mother, Louisa Maria Torrey Taft, was an independent woman with intellectual curiosity and liberal views on women's rights. She once wrote, "I do not want my son to be president. His is a judicial mind and he loves the law." On the other hand, his wife, Nellie, was an ambitious, intellectual and independent woman who pushed him to strive for more than a judicial career and put him on the presidential track to the White House.

Library of Congress

Will was born on September 15, 1857, in the Mount Auburn section of Cincinnati, OH. His father, Alphonso Taft, was a leader in the Republican Party and a career diplomat. He was a stern, reserved man who kept his emotions under rigid control. The elder Taft insisted that his children extend themselves to the fullest. "Mediocrity will not do, Will," he complained when his son stood fifth in a large class. Despite his father, Will had a happy, stimulating childhood with his five siblings in a home full of love and affection.

When he entered Woodward High School, Will had already reached his full height, and his powerful physique won him a reputation of a wrestler and fighter to be feared. His father even boasted to heavyweight boxing champion, John L. Sullivan, that he believed, "My Will is a better man." Will also did well in all his academic subjects, graduating second in his class with a four-year grade point average of 91.5 out of 100. However, William lived in constant fear of not meeting his parents' expectations no matter how well he performed. According to some scholars, Taft's large variations in his body weight stemmed from his social and family anxieties.

Following in his father's footsteps, Will entered Yale in 1874. He was a fun-loving, popular student, representing the freshman class in intramural wrestling. Despite his size, he was very light on his feet and an excellent dancer. He took prizes in mathematics and public speaking and was tapped by Skull and Bones, the ultimate symbol of success at Yale.

Artist Concept:

Taft was a very good athlete in his youth. Since he was the first president to throw out the opening pitch of the Major League Baseball season, the artist portrays him shaking off the catcher's sign and preparing to throw the "heater." Taft thought of himself in his prime, regardless of a few extra pounds.

Sculptor: Lee Leuning | Benefactor: BankWest

In 1878, 20-year-old William graduated as salutatorian in a class of 132 and made Phi Beta Kappa. However, his parents expressed disappointment in Will since he failed to graduate at the very top of his class.

Taft met Helen "Nellie" Herron in 1879 at a bobsledding party. They dated off and on until he proposed in April 1885. William, 28, married Nellie, 25, on June 19, 1886. She was an extremely ambitious woman who had wanted to be the country's first lady since childhood and pushed Taft into an office he didn't want. Taft was a loving husband, and, when his wife suffered a stroke two months after entering the White House, he spent two hours a day for the next year teaching her how to speak again.

Of Note:
The baseball behind Taft's back.

Before becoming president, Taft occupied a series of appointed positions such as governor of the Philippines and secretary of war. Like most other men who rose to the presidency without working their way up, he was ill-equipped to cope with political bosses, patronage and pleasing the public. In fact, Taft hated politics. During his life, he ran for only one elective office—the presidency. Given a choice, he much preferred the judiciary. All he wanted was to be a Supreme Court justice.

Before his inauguration in 1909 (which coincided with a winter storm), he joked, "I always said it would be a cold day when I got to be president of the United States."

Theodore Roosevelt was the main force behind Taft entering the race for president. After Taft won, Roosevelt left on a year-long safari to Africa to allow Taft to have some "breathing room." When he returned in 1910, Roosevelt severely criticized Taft for abandoning his own progressive policies. Many believe that Roosevelt's outcries were more a result of his deep beliefs that no one could run the country as well as he could. The break that he caused in their friendship lasted for many years. When Taft heard of Roosevelt's attacks on him, a reporter found the president with his head in his hands. Looking up, he said in a despairing voice, "Roosevelt was my closest friend." Unable to control himself any longer, he burst into tears.

Taft had a moderate view of presidential power, and he believed that the president should not exercise powers beyond those explicitly authorized by the Constitution. Taft believed that Roosevelt's progressive causes were outside the parameters of the role of president.

Taft was a warmhearted and kind man who wanted to be loved as a person and to be respected for his judicial temperament. It was his temperament that caused most of his problems as a political leader. He had little talent for leadership. He was inactive and typically ate a dozen eggs, a pound of bacon and mounds of pancakes for breakfast, which left him sluggish and prone to fall asleep during cabinet meetings, church services and social events. Biographers agree that his gigantic appetite reflected psychological tensions within himself that he never resolved.

Knowing that he had no chance of winning a second term, Taft spent no time campaigning. Because he was so upset over his friend's betrayal, speculation was that he stayed in the race, though, to make sure Roosevelt didn't win either.

The Tafts had many "firsts" to contribute to the presidential legacy. Taft was the first president to own his own automobile. He was the first president to play golf. However, he was too fat to bend down and place the ball on the tee, so his caddy had to do it for him. Being a huge sports fan with a love of baseball since childhood, Taft began the long-standing tradition of being the first president to throw out the first ball to open the Major League Baseball season.

The couple also was the last to keep their own cow. Taft liked milk so much that he brought his cow, Mooly, to the White House. Mooly was replaced then by Pauline, the last cow to graze on the White House lawn. With the admission of Arizona and New Mexico to the union, Taft was the first U. S. president to serve the 48 contiguous states and was the only president to go on to serve as chief justice of the Supreme Court. Even after his death, Taft was the first former president to be buried in Arlington National Cemetery. Nellie made her own lasting impression on the city of Washington when she arranged for the planting of 3,000 Japanese cherry trees along the Tidal Basin.

Rumor has it that Taft, weighing in at 335 pounds, got stuck in the White House bathtub and had to be pried out. He then had an oversized version (7' long x 41" wide) installed that could accommodate four normal-sized men. The president's weight made him the target of many "fat man" jokes. One story lauded Taft as one of the most polite men in Washington: "One day he gave up his seat on a streetcar to three women."

Taft even enjoyed a laugh at his own expense. While visiting Japan, Taft took a rickshaw to the temples high in the mountains. "The road was steep and got steeper," Taft recalled. "I had one 'pusher' in addition to the rickshaw man when I began, another joined when we were halfway up, and it seemed to me that when we struck the last hill, the whole village was engaged in the final push . . . The Japanese gathered in crowds about me, smiling and enjoying the prospect of so much flesh and size." When serving as governor-general of the Philippines, Taft once telegraphed Secretary of War Elihu Root, "Took long horseback ride today; feeling fine." Root cabled back, "How is the horse?"

In 1921, President Taft's lifelong dream was finally achieved when President Warren Harding appointed him as chief justice of the Supreme Court, a time he proclaimed as the happiest time of his life. He served the court well for nine years, until he became ill in February of 1930 and retired. On March 8, 1930, Taft died from complications of heart disease. His funeral was the first presidential funeral to be broadcast on the radio.

Supreme Court Justice Louis Brandeis probably summarized Taft's life best when he said, "It's very difficult for me to understand how a man who is so good as chief justice could have been so bad as president."

Woodrow Wilson

Most historians rank Woodrow Wilson among the five most important American presidents, along with George Washington, Abraham Lincoln, Theodore Roosevelt and Franklin Roosevelt. Wilson's father was a Presbyterian minister, and his mother was the daughter of a Presbyterian minister. As a result, his deep religious beliefs followed him throughout his life. He believed in providence and predestination and that God had preordained him to be president. As president, he dreamed of creating a lasting world peace where countries solved their problems through discussion and not violence.

Harris & Ewing Collection at the Library of Congress

Thomas Woodrow Wilson, who would later drop his first name, was born in Staunton, VA, on December 28, 1856. He was the third of four children born to the Reverend Joseph Ruggles Wilson and Janet (Jessie) Woodrow Wilson. Jessie was a loving companion to Wilson's father and a devoted mother to her children. Later in life, Wilson described himself as a "mama's boy" who had clung to his mother's apron strings. Joseph Wilson not only stressed the love of God but the love of learning to his children. Young Woodrow once said that he looked no further than his own father for a hero.

At the age of five, the Wilson family moved to Augusta, GA. There, he witnessed the horrors of the Civil War, and he never forgot the destruction he saw firsthand. During the war, the Wilson children were taught by their parents. Historians now believe that young Woodrow may have had difficulties learning to read because of weak eyesight and dyslexia. In fact, he was not able to read until the age of nine. Through persistence, Wilson finally mastered reading, and learning became one of the greatest loves of his life.

His parents believed that their son would follow in his father's footsteps as a Presbyterian minister, but Woodrow believed that God had chosen him to govern. He believed that he was destined to guide the United States to a lasting peace with the tragedy of the Civil War still fresh in his mind.

At the age of 16, Woodrow entered Davidson College in North Carolina. Whether

Artist Concept: ....

Wilson is depicted surrounded by symbols of his two passions—the academic robes draped over a pedestal and the papers of one serving in the highest post in the land.

Sculptor: James Michael Maher | Benefactor: GCC Dakotah Company

it was poor health or homesickness, young Wilson did not do well at college, and his mother encouraged him to return home to study. In 1875, at the age of 19, Wilson entered Princeton University. There, he thrived in the academic community, later referring to his time at Princeton as his "magical years." He studied government, economics and literature, preparing himself for his goal to govern. He even handed out name cards he had made for himself, declaring "Thomas Woodrow Wilson, Senator from Virginia."

In 1879, he moved on to the University of Virginia to study the law but found it dull and tiresome. Although he dropped out of law school, he continued his study of law at home and was admitted to the bar in 1882. He began to practice law, although he never received an actual law degree. Wilson believed that he was on the next step toward his dream of a life in politics.

During a trip to Rome in April 1883, 28-year-old Woodrow met a 25-year-old young woman named Ellen Louise Axson. Woodrow described her as a "noble and good" woman with ". . . lots of life and fun in her." Ellen was a nurturing woman, caring for her siblings and ailing father after the death of her mother. She loved art, music and literature, and hoped for a career as a painter until she fell in love with Woodrow. They soon became engaged but didn't marry until June 24, 1885.

When the political opportunities did not present themselves, Wilson decided that he would return to school to study government and political science. He entered Johns Hopkins University in 1883, and Wilson received a doctoral degree in history and political science in 1886. In fact, he was the only president to earn a doctorate, making him the most educated president so far. He got his first teaching assignment at Bryn Mawr, which was an all-women's college outside Philadelphia for a salary of $1,500 a year. However, he looked at women's education as less than men's education and feared that teaching women would make his mind lazy.

In April 1886, the first of three daughters was born to Woodrow and Ellen Wilson. In 1888, Wilson went to teach at Wesleyan University in Middletown, CT, where Wilson began his political writing. In 1890, he was asked to teach law at Princeton. His excellent teaching reputation followed him, and half the students at Princeton signed up to study under him. He was a popular professor, spending time speaking informally with his students late into the night. He hired many new professors, making smaller class sizes for better dialogue among teachers and students. Eventually, he was promoted to president in 1902.

An old tradition at Princeton involved the university's eating clubs. The wealthy students segregated themselves from the other students. Wilson considered this snobbery and bad for student life. He tried to abolish these clubs but met with outrage by the students. Wilson was furious at the dissension and left Princeton after eight years of teaching. This proved to be a perfect timing for Wilson's political aspirations.

In 1910, the Democratic Party was looking for a gubernatorial candidate for governor of New Jersey. Wilson accepted the offer to be the party's candidate if he did not have to return any favors. His earlier writings were against the favoritism of party bosses and big business interests on the political scene. He was committed to reform of the political system.

Newly elected Governor Wilson worked tirelessly to pass reform bills, making the monopolies of big businesses illegal in New Jersey. He worked to control utility and railroad prices and established a workman's compensation program. He made speeches on behalf of the "common man" who was being exploited by big business. Always working for progressive change, Wilson once described a conservative as "one who makes no changes and consults his grandmother when in doubt."

His passions for the average American came to the attention of the 1912 Democratic Party. They were looking for a candidate to enter the presidential race against incumbent Republican President William Howard Taft and third-party candidate Theodore Roosevelt. Taft and Roosevelt split the Republican vote, and Wilson won the election with a little less than 42 percent of the vote. He was inaugurated on March 4, 1913.

As president, Wilson golfed regularly for exercise, but he found little pleasure in a game he defined as "an ineffectual attempt to put an elusive ball into an obscure hole with implements ill-adapted to the purpose." His average for 18 holes was about 115 strokes.

Ellen proved to be a devoted wife to Woodrow and an activist in social issues of the time, lobbying Congress to fund cleanup of the slum areas in the District of Columbia. However, Ellen suffered from Bright's disease (a fatal kidney disease) and died in the White House on August 6, 1914, asking her physician to tell Wilson that she hoped he would marry again. Wilson was so devastated by her death that he confided to an aide that he hoped he would be assassinated. Later that same year though, Wilson married a wealthy young widow named Edith Bolling Galt. The second Mrs. Wilson was considered one of the country's most influential first ladies.

Wilson was re-elected in 1916. After the election, he concluded that America could not remain neutral in World War I and asked Congress for a declaration of war on Germany on April 2, 1917. As first lady, Mrs. Wilson observed "gasless Sundays," "meatless Mondays" and "wheatless Tuesdays" to set an example for the federal rationing effort. She also had sheep grazing on the White House lawn rather than mowing, and she auctioned off their wool to benefit the Red Cross.

As president, Wilson contracted influenza during the epidemic of 1918 and suffered acute asthma attacks that deprived him of sleep and sapped his strength. On October 2, 1919, he suffered a stroke, paralyzing his left side and slurring his speech. Mrs. Wilson stayed at the president's side, screening his visitors and mail.

On February 1, 1920, Wilson uttered, "I am a broken piece of machinery. When the machinery is broken . . ." He fell silent, then added, "I am ready." These were his last words. Two days later, on February 3, 1920, Wilson died, holding his wife's hand.

Warren G. Harding

The brief, scandal-ridden presidential administration of Warren Gamaliel Harding stands as a black mark in American history. Following Harding's inauguration, H. L. Mencken wrote a column assessing the new president: "No other such a complete and dreadful nitwit is to be found in the pages of American history."

Harris & Ewing Collection at the Library of Congress

Harding was the epitome of a rural and small-town American. Born on November 2, 1865, on the family farm near Blooming Grove in Ohio, he was the oldest of six children of George and Phoebe Harding, who were both physicians.

He and his five siblings attended a one-room schoolhouse where he learned to read, write and spell from the McGuffey's Readers. From early childhood, Warren was haunted by rumors that the Hardings were of African-American blood. These rumors continued on throughout Warren's adulthood, although there was no evidence to substantiate this rumor, which may have been started by an angry neighbor.

At 14, Warren entered Ohio Central College where he excelled in debating and composition and achieved distinction for editing the campus newspaper. He graduated with a B. S. degree in 1882. After college, he taught in a country school outside Marion, OH, for one term, earning $30 a month. He then tried his hand at law, insurance sales and journalism for the local newspaper called the *Marion Star*. However, he preferred shooting pool and playing poker with the town sports. In 1884, he raised $300 and purchased the nearly defunct newspaper and had moderate success over the next five years. Even then, a rival newspaper competing for advertising dollars, once hinted that Harding was part black.

In 1890, Warren met Florence "Flossie" Mabel Kling DeWolfe, a divorcee who was the daughter of a wealthy banker with one son. She was a headstrong, dowdy woman, who was somewhat masculine. From the first moment she met "Wurr'n" (as she pronounced his name), she chased after him. Harding tried to avoid her advances, but he finally gave in and found himself engaged to be married. Flossie's father strongly opposed the marriage,

Artist Concept:

Due to the Teapot Dome scandal and corruption within his cabinet, Harding had a public relations problem during his term. At the time, a photograph of him and his dog, Laddie, was published to make the president seem more likeable. This was the artist's inspiration.

Sculptor: John Lopez | Benefactors: Brant C. and Melissa E. Grote

warning his daughter not to marry into what he called "the black-blooded" Harding family. Ignoring her father's warnings, Flossie, 30, married Warren, 25, at his home in Marion, OH, on July 8, 1891.

Unfortunately, they had an unhappy marriage. They had no children, and Harding neglected her, preferring the friendships of his poker pals and the arms of other women. Still, Flossie's managerial skills helped him build his newspaper into a financial success.

In 1915, Harding won the election for the senator from Ohio. His record as a senator was one of the poorest, missing many critical votes on women's rights, prohibition and the League of Nations. "Harding desperately sought approval all his life," wrote biographer Andrew Sinclair. "He hated to be forced to decide on matters that might antagonize people." Harding himself acknowledged his indecisive nature when he revealed that his father had said, "Warren, it's a good thing you wasn't born a gal, because you'd be in the family way all the time. You can't say 'No'."

Beginning in 1905, Harding began a 15-year affair with Carrie Phillips, the wife of a longtime friend, James Phillips. Carrie was a tall, attractive woman who was 10 years younger than Harding. The affair seemed perfect until Carrie began pressing Harding to leave his wife. When he refused, Carrie left her husband and took her daughter to Berlin, Germany. During her stay abroad, she became very attached to the country and became an outspoken advocate for Germany when she returned to America. As the U. S. moved closer to war with Germany, Carrie threatened to expose their affair unless Senator Harding voted against a declaration of war. Harding called her bluff and voted for the declaration. Carrie backed off, and the affair continued until Harding won the Republican presidential nomination. To avoid a scandal, the Republican National Convention sent Carrie and her husband (who then knew of the affair) on a free, slow trip to Japan and gave them $20,000. They also received monthly payments in exchange for their silence. These payoffs continued until Harding's death.

Even while seeing Carrie, Harding was registering into hotels with his "niece," Nan Britton, a cute blond more than 30 years younger than he. The affair began in 1917 when Nan wrote to Senator Harding, asking him to help her find a job in Washington, D. C. Harding got her a position as a secretary at the U. S. Steel Corporation. Nan gave birth to Harding's child, Elizabeth Ann Christian, on October 22, 1919. Although Harding never saw his daughter, he paid Nan generous child support hand delivered by secret service agents. The couple actually continued the affair while Harding was president, making love in a closet near the president's office in the White House. Upon his death, Nan tried unsuccessfully to establish a trust fund from Harding's estate. Failing that, she wrote the best seller, *The President's Daughter*, which was dedicated "to all unwed mothers, and to their innocent children whose fathers are usually not known to the world."

In 1920, Harding was nominated by the Republican Party as their dark-horse candidate. He was a bitterly contested candidate, competing against three other nominees who were vastly more qualified. Finally, party leaders settled on Harding because he had no strikes against him. Unlike usual presidential campaigns, Harding chose to campaign from his front porch in Marion, OH. He greeted thousands of people, speaking informally to them about his love for humanity, his patriotism and his belief in the Republican Party. On election day, Harding won a landslide victory and was sworn in on March 4, 1921.

Between the election and the inauguration, Harding chose his cabinet. Some were close, political cronies; others represented various factions of the Republican Party. Although this was Harding's formal cabinet, much of the real business of his administration took place during the evening poker games and drinking parties in the White House.

Once in office, Harding admitted to his close friends that the job was beyond him, stating, "I am a man of limited talents, from a small town. I do not seem to grasp that I am President." Friends of Harding and Attorney General Harry Daugherty flocked from Ohio to Washington, looking for influential government jobs. This group soon became known as the "Ohio Gang," who bought and sold government appointments. There was never any evidence that Harding himself knew of these dealings. His friends merely knew that he would agree with their appointments in order to please them.

Scandals continued to plague Harding's presidency. Some members of his cabinet were unscrupulous politicians. Secretary of Interior Albert Fall sold the nation's oil reserves at Wyoming's Teapot Dome for personal gain. Thomas Miller was convicted of accepting bribes. Jess Smith, bagman for the operation and personal aide to Attorney General Daugherty, committed suicide. An aide to Charles Forbes, director of the Veterans Bureau, skimmed the proceeds from the sale of war surplus goods, earned fat kickbacks for purchasing government supplies at exorbitant prices and diverted alcohol and drugs from Veterans' hospitals to bootleggers and narcotics dealers. No evidence suggests that Harding personally profited from such crimes. In fact, Harding was once heard to say, "My God, this is a hell of a job! I have no trouble with my enemies. I can take care of my enemies all right. But my damn friends, my goddamn friends . . . they are the ones that keep me walking the floor nights."

On June 20, 1923, Harding set out on a cross-country "Voyage of Understanding" tour, hoping to meet ordinary folks and explain his administration's policies. Suffering from high blood pressure and an enlarged heart, the trip exhausted him. On July 27, he became ill, but his doctor dismissed it as a touch of food poisoning. The presidential train continued to San Francisco. He soon developed pneumonia, and when his nurse checked on him on the evening of August 2, she found his lifeless body. Doctors concluded he had suffered a heart attack. In 1930, a convicted swindler published a sensational book, *The Strange Death of President Harding*, suggesting Mrs. Harding had poisoned her husband as punishment for cheating on her or to spare him the indignity of impeachment (or both). Because Mrs. Harding refused an autopsy, the charges could not be disproved, but historians generally discount it. Most historians regard Harding as the worst president in the nation's history. In the end, it was not his corrupt friends, but rather Harding's own lack of vision that was most responsible for his tarnished legacy.

Calvin Coolidge

Calvin Coolidge's elevation to the presidency was not one of nomination, campaign or election-day outcomes. Instead, Vice-President Coolidge was awakened from a sound sleep by his father while visiting his childhood home on August 3, 1923. Having no telephone in this rural area of Plymouth Notch, VT, messengers from the White House had arrived at his father's home to notify Coolidge that President Warren G. Harding had died. It was necessary for the change of power to take place quickly, so the family dressed and gathered in the parlor. Coolidge's father, John, who was a notary public, administered the presidential oath by the light of a kerosene lamp. President Coolidge signed the oath in triplicate, then went back to sleep.

Lincoln Borglum Collection

Born on the Fourth of July, 1872, John Calvin Coolidge was the first-born child of John and Victoria Moor Coolidge in Plymouth Notch, VT. His boyhood home was a small cottage attached to a general store and post office where his father served as merchant, postmaster and tax collector. The family also maintained a farm where John and young Calvin worked the fields. The family and the community embraced the values of hard work, honesty, integrity and emotions kept in check. These traits were passed on from father to son. Calvin was a shy, quiet boy with red hair and freckles. He was a good student who loved the nature of Vermont and worked and played hard as a child.

When Calvin was three years old, his sister Abigail was born. His father was distant by nature, but Calvin was extremely close to both his mother and sister. Due to complications during Abigail's birth, Victoria's health became quite fragile. When Calvin was only 12 years old, a runaway horse injured his mother, and her health worsened. In March of 1885, Calvin was with his mother when she died. He described her death as "the greatest grief that can come to a boy." Coolidge carried a picture of his mother in his watchcase until he died.

The following year, John Coolidge enrolled Calvin in Black River Academy, which was a private school 12 miles from home. For the next four years, Calvin studied history,

Artist Concept:

Coolidge's statue is the only site-specific one. He appears to be waving a welcome to Rapid City visitors and is shown with a big Stetson hat and cowboy boots. He is standing next to a saddle made by local saddle-maker Bud Duhamel.

Sculptor: John Lopez | Benefactors: Don Herrmann, Constance Lane and Rapid City Journal

mathematics, literature, Latin and Greek. In his senior year, tragedy struck again when his beloved sister Abigail died. Calvin never totally recovered from the death of his mother or sister.

In 1891, Calvin entered Amherst College. His shyness and lack of social skills made it difficult to make friends. During his first two years of college, his grades were mediocre. With encouragement from his father, his grades improved. He became more sociable and was accepted as a fraternity brother. He ultimately graduated with honors.

After graduation in 1895, Calvin set a goal to "be of some use in the world" and entered law school. He proved to be an excellent law student and passed the Massachusetts bar examination in only 20 months. After seven months at a law firm, he struck out on his own. He also became active in local Republican politics. His reputation for honesty and hard work led to a successful law practice and the attention of the political pundits.

Near the boardinghouse where Calvin was living was the Clarke Institute for the Deaf. It was here that Calvin noticed a beautiful young teacher named Miss Grace Anna Goodhue. Friends of Calvin and Grace felt this a strange courtship as Cal had the reputation of being shy and withdrawn while Grace was charming and spirited. Coolidge earned the nickname "Silent Cal," known for his minimal conversations and brevity of expression. Even his proposal to Grace was to the point. "I am going to be married to you," he announced. Cheerfully, Grace accepted, and they were married October 4, 1905.

Their first son, John, was born in 1906, and Calvin, Jr., was born in 1908. By then, Calvin was heavily involved in politics. His campaign style fit his personality. He walked up to people and simply said, "I want your vote. I need it. I shall appreciate it."

He went on to become governor of Massachusetts. While governor, Coolidge worked for women's rights and was pleased when women earned the right to vote in 1920. Coolidge received the attention of the National Republican Party after he took a stand against the Boston police when they called a strike against the city. Taking charge, Coolidge ordered the national guardsmen to maintain order. Coolidge then fired the striking policemen, insisting, "There is no right to strike against the public safety by anybody, anywhere, any time!" As a result of his firm stand, Coolidge emerged as a national hero.

In 1920, Coolidge's popularity elevated him to the candidate of vice president with Warren G. Harding. Harding and Coolidge ran a successful campaign for the White House. On March 4, 1921, they were sworn in as the 29th president and vice president.

"Silent Cal" conducted his vice presidency in the same tight-lipped manner he was well-known for. When the governor of Massachusetts asked Coolidge how he was able to see so many more people in a given day, Coolidge responded, "You talk back."

A popular story about Coolidge was when a society woman, sitting next to him at a dinner party, said, "You must talk to me, Mr. Coolidge. I made a bet that I could get more than two words out of you." Coolidge replied, "You lose." Alice Roosevelt Longworth, Theodore Roosevelt's daughter, liked to say that he had been weaned on a dill pickle with a personality to match his sour appearance."

Calvin Coolidge

In his role as vice president, Coolidge's responsibilities were conducted in his usual low-key fashion. While attending Senate and cabinet meetings, his contributions were more of listening than speech-making. In 1923, President Harding fell ill and suffered a fatal heart attack and so began the presidency of Calvin Coolidge.

After becoming president, Coolidge discovered there was corruption connected with the Harding presidency like the Teapot Dome scandal, which involved the bribery of the secretary of interior to create private development of government oil reserves in Wyoming. Coolidge quickly resolved this by firing the interior secretary, sending him to prison and fining him $100,000. This swift resolution of corruption set the tone for Coolidge's administration and earned him the respect of the nation. Coolidge's philosophy was "four-fifths of all our troubles in this life would disappear if we would only sit down and keep still."

Silent Cal was also famous for his odd habits. He was often spotted in a rocking chair on the front porch of the White House playing the harmonica. He had a number of household pets including a raccoon, Rebecca, that he walked on a leash. He was as frugal with expenses as he was with his words, known for serving small portions of food at White House dinners. Water was served in paper cups. He also tried to raise chickens in the backyard of the White House.

Throughout 1923 and 1924, America continued to prosper. In June 1924, during the first national political convention ever broadcast on radio, Coolidge received the nomination of his Republican Party. While campaigning for re-election, the president received news that his 16-year-old son, Calvin, Jr., had developed a critical infection. With the president by his side, young Calvin died on July 7. It was said that Coolidge never recovered from the grief of losing his son.

On November 4, 1924, President Coolidge won re-election by a two-to-one margin. The country continued to prosper over the next four years during the "Roaring Twenties." However, Coolidge felt it was socially unacceptable for Grace to fly on a plane, drive a car, ride a horse, wear pants, cut her hair short or dance in public.

Before the end of his term, Coolidge decided not to run for re-election. While visiting Rapid City, SD, he jokingly told a reporter his reason was "there's no chance for advancement." Many historians believe that the president had foreseen the recklessness of Wall Street investments and did not want to be in office when the stock market bubble burst. Others say that he never recovered from the death of his son. In October 1929, the stock market crashed resulting in the Great Depression.

On January 5, 1933, at the age of 60, Calvin Coolidge died quietly and alone of a sudden heart attack. He was remembered by a nation for his honesty, sense of dignity, dry wit and curious habits.

Herbert Hoover

Herbert Hoover was known as "The Great Humanitarian" and "The Great Engineer." However, young "Bertie," as he was called, had a life of hardship and tragedy before he reached the age of nine. Soon after his birth, he was plagued with asthma. At one time, he fell very ill, and his family covered him with a bed sheet, believing him to be dead. Only after the arrival of a doctor was baby Herbert revived. His grandmother announced to the assembled family that "God has a great work for that boy to do; that is why he was brought back to life."

Library of Congress

Born on August 10, 1874, in West Branch, IA, Herbert was the second son born to Jesse and Hulda Minthorn Hoover. The Quaker religion was the center of their life. Hoover later said that their religious discipline gave him a belief in the worth of the individual and a "strong training in patience" throughout the rest of his life. Jesse had a prosperous farm machinery business, and his mother held prayer meetings in their home. When Herbert was six years old, his father died at the age of 34. His mother then began to take in sewing jobs and renting rooms in their home to support her children. Four years later, while conducting a revival meeting, Hulda was stricken with typhoid fever and died at the age of 35. This left Herbert, his older brother, Tad, and his younger sister, May, orphaned. The three children were separated and lived with various members of the family throughout the state. When Hoover was older, he was sometimes described as being distant, reserved and even unfeeling. It is not difficult to understand his personality when studying his childhood.

In 1885, Dr. John and Laura Minthorn (Herbert's aunt and uncle) lost their only son and asked Bertie to come and live with them in Newberg, OR. There, Herbert (now called "Bert") enrolled in the Friends Pacific Academy. In 1888, the family moved to Salem, OR, where his Uncle John went into the real estate business. Fifteen-year-old Bert worked for his uncle, and John began encouraging him to attend college for engineering. However, Quaker schools did not teach engineering, and Stanford—his college of choice—required

Artist Concept:

Hoover is shown standing on a platform that symbolizes his contributions to people around the world. The base of this statue includes Hoover Dam, which is a result of Hoover's engineering abilities, and a chaff of wheat, which represents Hoover's shipments of food for starving millions in Europe.

Sculptor: James Michael Maher| Benefactors: Arthur and Sarah Ludwick

an entrance examination. Because of his lack of formal education and poor grades, Herbert failed the entrance exam. However, the test administrator saw something in him and suggested a tutor as he prepared to take the test again. Hoover took the entrance exam again and passed. To pay for his room, board and textbooks, Hoover took a job at the college and cared for the boardinghouse's horses. Bert took classes in mechanical engineering and geology. He found that he had a special talent in the area of geology and became involved in government geology projects, which eventually led him into the mining industry.

Hoover became known less for his academics and more for his organizational skills. Even in college sports, he chose to manage the school's baseball team rather than play. When former president Benjamin Harrison attended a Stanford baseball game, Hoover insisted the president purchase a ticket. Once, when a ballplayer asked for new shoes, Bert demanded to see the old ones first. He decided the player only needed new laces, and that was all he provided.

In his senior year, Bert's professor asked him to tutor the school's first female geology student named Lou Henry. Fascinated by her independence, her love of the outdoors and a common interest in geology, a romance soon developed.

Hoover graduated from Stanford with a degree in geology. He headed for the gold fields of California where he became a night laborer deep inside a mine. With the salary of $14 for a 70-hour week, he eventually saved enough money to leave the darkness of the mines to seek a better profession. His education was finally taken into account, and he was hired as an assistant to a mining engineer in San Francisco. At that time, Herbert was able to reunite with his brother, Tad, and sister, May. For the first time since their mother's death, they all lived under the same roof until his job took him elsewhere. His employer recognized his engineering talents, and Hoover was given the task to develop gold mines in Australia at a salary of $5,000 a year at the age of 22 with less than two years experience.

In May 1897, Hoover traveled to Australia where he was successful in locating and developing profitable gold mines. Soon his salary increased to $12,500. However, Hoover became homesick, especially for Lou. When offered a chance to explore into China with the mine, he sent two telegrams. One was to his employer accepting his new position, and the other was to Lou, asking her to marry him. Lou accepted his proposal, and they were married in Monterey, CA, on February 10, 1899. The next day they left for northern China.

Hoover worked closely with the Chinese emperor to develop the country's mines. Unlike many other western developers in China who made profits off China's resources, Hoover wanted to create a mining law to keep the mines under Chinese governmental control. However, the Boxer Rebellion began against Western developers when Chinese nationalists rebelled against colonial control of their nation, trapping 800 Westerners in the city of Tientsin. Hoover spearheaded the Westerner's efforts in building barricades around their residential section of the city, while Lou volunteered in the hospital. Legend holds that, during the ensuing month-long siege, Hoover rescued some Chinese children caught in the crossfire of combat. The Hoovers stayed on to help the Chinese until peace was restored.

Upon his return to England in 1901, he was made part owner in the global mining company at the young age of 27.

The Hoover's first son, Herbert, Jr., was born in 1903, and their second son, Allan, was born in 1907. The entire Hoover family traveled around the world five times in five years. By 1908, Hoover decided to leave the company and start his own business, which reorganized failing companies and found new mining prospects. His business experience in dealing with large companies and vast amounts of money made him very successful, and his wealth grew. As a result, he became known as "The Great Engineer."

Hoover developed strong beliefs in American democracy after observing the abject poverty of China and the privilege of British aristocracy. Rising from a poor orphan to a millionaire, Hoover knew firsthand the American dream.

The Hoovers were in London when World War I broke out. He immediately arranged to have thousands of U. S. citizens, who were stranded in Europe, sent back to America. He then initiated and supervised the feeding and clothing of thousands of Europeans. President Woodrow Wilson soon recognized Hoover's humanitarian efforts and called him back to the U. S. to administer food distribution to the U. S. military and the Allied troops in Europe. As the head of the American Relief Administration, Hoover managed the provision of food to 300 million people across Europe.

In 1921, Republican President Warren Harding appointed Hoover as secretary of commerce. He continued to be active in the area of disaster relief, organizing aid to Russia and flood relief for the Mississippi River during the 1920s. Because of these efforts, Hoover became known as "The Great Humanitarian."

When President Calvin Coolidge chose not to run for re-election in 1927, Hoover was waiting in the wings to seek the Republican nomination for president. Although he had the unique distinction of never having run for public office before, he easily won the nomination and the election. However, "The Great Humanitarian" and "The Great Engineer" was not as successful as president. The Great Depression reached its heights soon after Hoover became president. Although the Depression had begun before Hoover took office, it was Hoover who was blamed for the national despair that followed.

He left the political arena in 1933 but continued to be active in humanitarian activities, advising President Harry Truman on relief in Europe after World War II. President Dwight Eisenhower even used Hoover's organizational skills in streamlining government operations in 1953.

Hoover did not formally retire until the age of 81. After surviving intestinal cancer in 1962 and being virtually blind and deaf near the end, he died on October 20, 1964, at the age of 90.

Franklin D. Roosevelt

At the age of five, young Franklin D. Roosevelt accompanied his father, James, to the Oval Office of President Grover Cleveland. His father was there to decline an offer to become ambassador to the Netherlands. Disturbed by James's decision, Cleveland told the small boy, "Little man, I am making a strange wish for you. It is that you may never be president of the United States." Little did Cleveland know that this small boy would grow up to be the country's only four-term president or that he would hand down unprecedented decisions that would change the social climate of the country during the Great Depression and during times of war.

Library of Congress

Franklin Delano Roosevelt was an only child born on January 30, 1882, into wealth and prestige. The Roosevelt name stood out in the financial and political arenas. His father had ownership in railroads, coal and other investments. Franklin's mother, Sara Delano, also came from a wealthy shipping family. At the age of four, his shy, distant cousin, Eleanor, visited the Roosevelts. His rough play terrified her. It is hard to believe that these two very different children would later reunite, date and marry.

Franklin did not attend public school. Living in affluence, he was taught by tutors. Franklin spent his youth on his father's large estate, unaware of the poor and starving people in tenements just miles away from his home. James, as it turned out, believed in helping the poor but not through government assistance. He thought the rich—not the government—owed a duty to the poor.

As a student, Franklin read books shelf by shelf with a remarkable ability to remember everything he read. Once, while Sara was reading to her son, he seemed preoccupied with his stamp collection. She became angry at his lack of attention until he recited back to her, word for word, what she had just read. "Mama," he said, "I would be ashamed of myself if I couldn't do at least two things at once."

As Franklin grew to young adulthood, his cousin, Teddy Roosevelt, rose through the

Artist Concept: ....

Roosevelt is depicted as he stood and presented himself to the nation during his "day which will live in infamy" speech. Roosevelt's stance shows him gripping the podium to steady himself because of the effects of polio. His determination to project the image of strength despite his physical restraints is evident. Sculptor: Edward Hlavka | Benefactors: The Furniture Mart, Freed's Furniture and Anonymous donor

Republican ranks—first as a New York state legislator and then as assistant secretary of the navy. Teddy was then elected as governor of New York in 1898, and, in 1900, he became the vice president under President William McKinley.

In the fall of 1896, Franklin entered the elite school of Groton Academy at the age of 14. In the fall of 1899, Franklin returned to his home to inform his father that he wanted to go to Annapolis. James was in very poor health and reminded Franklin that he would soon be responsible for the Roosevelt family and fortune. Deeply disappointed, Franklin turned to his ailing father and said "All right, papa, Harvard it is." After his freshman year, Franklin learned of the assassination of McKinley, elevating Teddy to the presidency.

Being related to the new president, Franklin and Eleanor renewed their earlier friendship while attending parties at the White House. In 1903, while at a Harvard football game together, Franklin proposed to Eleanor. His mother tried to delay the marriage,

Of Note: **FDR with his leg braces.**

believing her handsome son could do better than Eleanor, who was known to the family as the "ugly duckling." However, they set a wedding date and married on March 17, 1905, with President Theodore Roosevelt walking his niece down the aisle.

Franklin studied law at Columbia and entered the big-money world of Wall Street, but he never gave up his dream for a political life. When approached by the Democrats to seek office, Roosevelt already had a clear plan for his political future—to follow his cousin's course to the White House. First, he would serve in the New York legislature and then become assistant secretary of the navy. The next step would be the governorship of New York.

In 1910, Franklin won a seat in the New York state senate. The Roosevelts and their three children (Anna, James and Elliot) moved to the state capital in Albany. In 1911, Roosevelt was planning for his re-election to the state senate when he was stricken with typhoid fever. He was confined to his bed, making campaigning impossible. Louis Howe, who advised Roosevelt throughout his political life, led a successful campaign that put Roosevelt in the New York state senate in 1911. Step one was accomplished!

While attending the 1913 inauguration of Democratic President Woodrow Wilson, Roosevelt was approached by Secretary of the Navy Josephus Daniels. Daniels asked Roosevelt, "How would you like to serve as my assistant secretary of the navy?" Step two was accomplished!

On April 2, 1917, following an attack of a German submarine on an American ship, President Wilson stood before Congress and said, "The world must be made safe for democracy." That prompted 35-year-old Roosevelt, now the father of five children, to submit his resignation to Wilson so that he could assume command of a ship as a naval officer, but the president would not accept it.

Unable to serve in the navy, Roosevelt chose to support the military in another way. He travelled the country, inspecting the readiness of American shipyards. At a Boston shipyard, Franklin asked that a newly built ship be turned over to the navy immediately. The supervisor refused, saying no ship would leave his yard until the navy paid for it. A few days later, the Marines appeared in the shipyard and ordered the supervisor, at gunpoint, to release the ship. The marines sailed out of the yard aboard the ship. Obviously, Franklin Roosevelt meant business.

In 1921, now a private citizen, Roosevelt took a position as vice president of a banking company and began a law practice. It was during this time that he was faced with a great personal challenge. One day, after a strenuous time of sailing and jogging with his family, he retired to bed, not feeling well. The next morning he awoke and tried to get up. His legs would not support him. He was diagnosed with polio, and Roosevelt never walked unassisted again. His physical limitations never stopped him though. For example, it was his strength of character that upheld him as he stood clutching to a podium, speaking these famous words after the bombing of Pearl Harbor: "The only thing we have to fear is fear itself."

In the election year of 1928, the Republicans nominated Herbert Hoover to run as the Republican candidate. The Democrats approached Al Smith, governor of New York, to run on the Democratic ticket. Knowing he could not run for re-election as governor and the bid for the president at the same time, Smith convinced a reluctant Roosevelt to run for the governor of New York. Although Smith lost the election, Roosevelt won his, and step three was accomplished!

In October of 1929, the prosperity of the previous years came to a crashing halt. Americans stood by helplessly as billions of dollars in paper profits vanished. While President Hoover did nothing to restore the lost prosperity, Roosevelt called in his advisors to establish new laws to provide jobs and food to the homeless and the poor. He taxed the rich to provide for the poor. In 1932, Roosevelt was nominated by the Democratic Party to run for the presidency. At the convention, Franklin told the delegates, "I pledge to you, I pledge to myself, to a new deal for the American people. A new deal. A new start."

Roosevelt went on to defeat Hoover in a landslide, and Roosevelt took the oath of office on March 4, 1933, and served as president until 1945. As Roosevelt's health and mobility worsened, Eleanor became "the eyes and the legs" of the president, visiting and relaying back to him the plight of the homeless, the poor and those deserving government support. It is said that, without Eleanor's contributions, Roosevelt would not have been as effective or as compassionate as he turned out to be.

In his 12 years as president, Roosevelt had to deal with the Great Depression and World War II. He instituted many social policies, including the New Deal's National Recovery Administration, Civilian Conservation Corps, Public Works Administration, Social Security Administration and the Federal Emergency Relief Administration. As a result of the war, defense spending created new jobs and set the stage for economic growth during the 1940s and 1950s.

Unfortunately, 30 days after Roosevelt began his fourth presidential term, an ailing Roosevelt suffered a massive stroke and died on April 12, 1945.

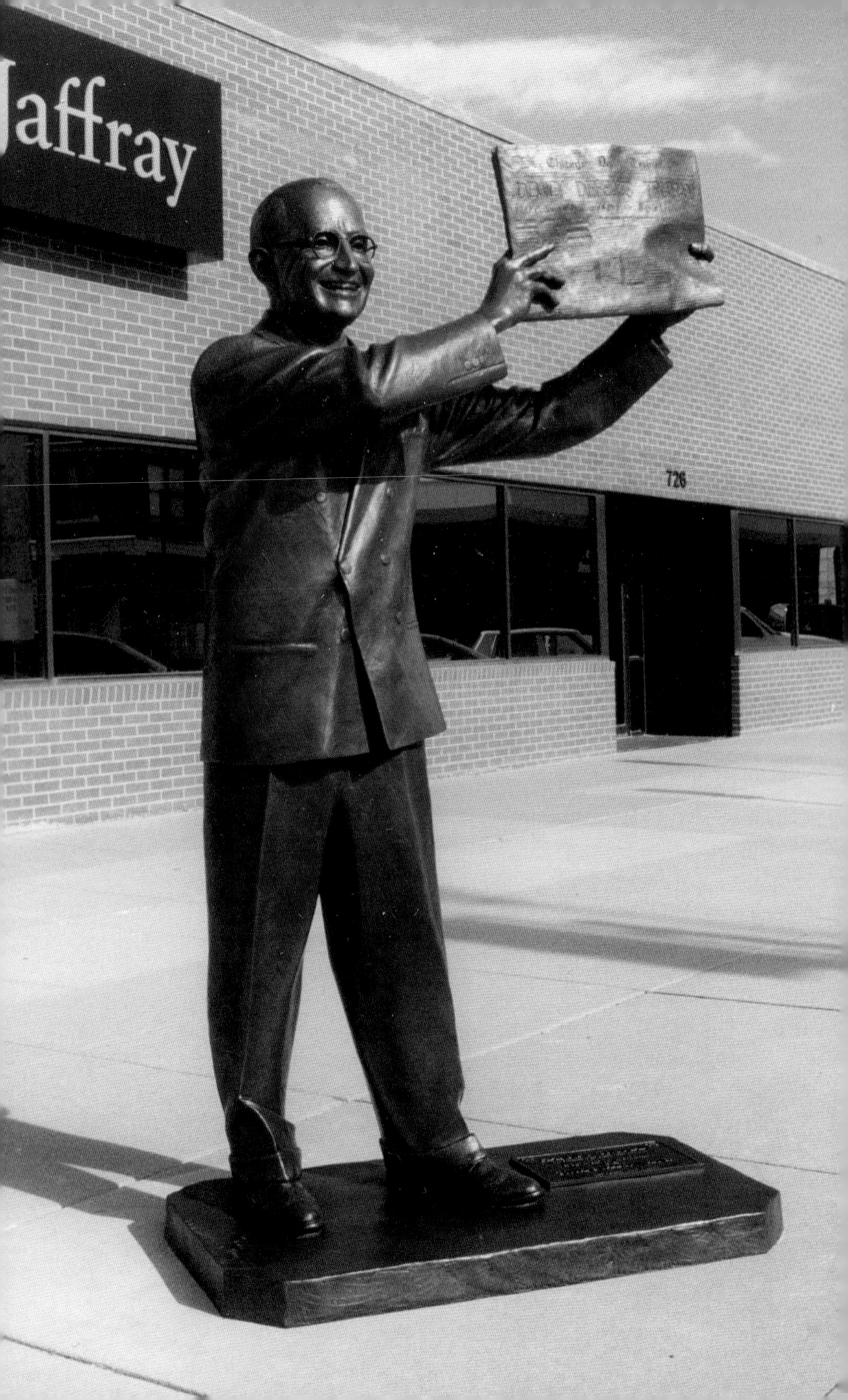
affray
726

Harry S. Truman

When Harry Truman awoke the morning after the 1948 presidential election, the *Chicago Daily Tribune* headlines read, "Dewey Defeats Truman." The polls and the media had all projected a decisive win by Republican presidential candidate Thomas E. Dewey. However, the final count gave President Harry Truman his second term as president of the United States by over two million votes. To this day, the famous photograph of Truman holding up the misinformed *Chicago Daily Tribune* is one of the most famous in presidential history.

Portrait by Greta Kempton

This event in Truman's life proved to be an amusing surprise, but there were other unexpected occurrences that were not so lighthearted. Late in the afternoon of April 12, 1945, then Vice-President Truman was called to the White House by President Franklin Roosevelt's press secretary. Upon his arrival, First Lady Eleanor Roosevelt told Truman that her husband had just died. The new president asked Mrs. Roosevelt if there was anything he could do for her. Her reply was, "Is there anything we can do for you . . . for you are the one in trouble now."

The son of John Anderson Truman and Martha Young Truman was born in Lamar, MO, on May 8, 1884. He was named "Harry" after his uncle, Harrison Young. His parents could not decide on a middle name for Harry. His father wanted him named after his own father, "Shippe," and his mother wanted to name him "Solomon" after her father. The final decision was to use the initial "S" out of respect for both grandfathers.

Harry was a very bright child who loved to read. His mother taught him at a very early age, and he was reading books by the age of five. At the age of six, Mrs. Truman enrolled Harry in Sunday School. It was there that he met a pretty little girl named Elizabeth Virginia Wallace, nicknamed "Bess." Truman later wrote, "It was right then that I knew she would be the love of my life." From the fifth grade on, Harry and Bess went to school together, and Bess went on to become Harry's wife of 53 years.

At the age of six, Harry was diagnosed with farsightedness and began wearing

Artist Concept: ···

Truman is shown displaying the Chicago Daily Tribune *newspaper the day after the presidential election of 1948. His big smile negates the headlines erroneously declaring his opponent the winner.*

Sculptor: James Michael Maher | Benefactors: Tom and Sharon Warner

eyeglasses. Bess was the more athletic of the two, while Harry loved reading, especially history. In fact, Harry and a friend once set a goal to read all 2,000 books in the town library, and they came very close. At the age of 13, Harry earned $3 a week cleaning a local drug store. He became a fine piano player and considered pursuing a career as a concert pianist.

Harry graduated from high school in 1901, but his father did not earn enough money from the family farm to finance Harry's college education. Instead, Harry worked odd jobs until returning to work in the family farm.

Bess lived across the street from Harry's aunt and uncle in Independence, MO. Bess and Harry resumed their friendship that soon blossomed into courtship. In 1917, Harry and Bess became engaged. That same year, the U. S. entered World War I, and Harry joined the Missouri National Guard as a recruiter. When the National Guard became part of the U. S. Army, Truman secretly memorized the eye chart in his desire to stay in the military service and joined the army.

Of Note: **Truman with the famous** *Chicago Daily Tribune* **edition.**

In 1918, he went to France and was promoted to captain and put in charge of Battery D, which was made up of Irish toughs from Kansas City. Captain Truman was a man of medium stature at 5' 10" tall and wore thick glasses, but Truman's leadership earned him the respect of his men. They described him as tough, brave and fair. He left the military with the rank of major.

Truman returned to the U. S. and, on June 28, 1919, was married to his beloved Bess, declaring it "the happiest day of my life."

Soon after, Harry and a friend opened a men's clothing store in Kansas City. By 1920, the economy was declining, and the company was forced to close. Despite the fact that his business partner filed bankruptcy, Truman repaid the $28,000 he owed within 12 years.

In 1922, friends approached Harry to run for political office. Harry agreed and was elected judge of eastern Jackson County in Missouri. Although failing to be re-elected in 1924, he won again in 1926 on a reputation of being an honest man in the divisive political climate of that time. Bess and Harry's only daughter, Margaret, was born during this time on February 17, 1924.

Truman then went on to win a senate seat in 1935. As a new senator, he seriously studied the railroad problems, and his recommendations were part of the Transportation Act of 1940. In 1940, Truman was also re-elected to the U. S. Senate.

In 1939, World War II broke out. As the U. S. began building up its armed forces, Truman personally investigated the stories of uncontrolled government spending. He formed an investigative committee to look into airplanes, ships, factories and food supplies. The Truman committee saved the country as much as $15 billion dollars. His hard work on this committee earned him the respect of the American people and the attention of President Franklin D. Roosevelt.

Roosevelt was running for his fourth term as president in 1944. He asked Truman to join him on the ticket, but Truman was clear on his desire to stay in the senate. After several refusals, Roosevelt shouted so loudly over the phone that Truman could hear him across the room. He said, "Well, you tell him if he wants to break up the Democratic party in the middle of the war, that's his responsibility." Truman got the message loud and clear. Roosevelt went on to win his fourth presidential term with Truman as his vice president. Less than three months later, on April 13, 1945, Roosevelt died suddenly, and Truman became president with little or no knowledge of the conflicts and trials that would befall him and this country.

On the first day of his presidency, Truman was informed of the atomic bomb, which was a highly secretive weapon that held the future of the world in its grip. On May 8, 1945, President Truman went on the radio to inform the American people that Germany had surrendered after a six-year-long war. However, the U. S. was still at war with Japan, and all indicators predicted that Japan was not going to quit. Truman had a difficult decision to make. Continued conflicts with Japan would result in massive losses of American lives. On July 26, 1945, Truman asked Japan to surrender. Receiving no reply from Japan, Truman gave the order to drop the atomic bomb on Hiroshima on August 6, 1945. Still, the Japanese did not surrender. On August 9, a second atomic bomb was dropped on Nagasaki. Less than one day later, Japan did surrender.

Truman accomplished many notable things in his presidency. For instance, he recognized the importance of a platform on which all nations of the world could voice their differences. After much debate, the United Nations was established. Domestically, Truman proposed new laws in the areas of civil rights, a national health plan system and federal aid for education. Unfortunately, the American people were not prepared to accept these new laws, and the post-war economy was out of control. Immediately after the war was over, the railroad workers and the coal miners went on strike. Truman appealed to their duty to their country. When this did not work, he threatened to draft the striking workers, and the strike ended quickly.

Truman had a sign on his desk in the oval office that simply said, "The Buck Stops Here!" He believed that "The President must make his own decisions. He cannot pass the buck up or down."

During his presidency, Truman was forced to deal with the suspicion of communists in America by Senator Joe McCarthy, the breakout of war between North and South Korea and the Cold War with Russia and communism in Eastern Europe.

At 68, Truman decided not to run for re-election in 1952. Harry and Bess returned to their home in Kansas City, MO. He died on December 26, 1972, at the age of 88. It was once said by a childhood friend that "Harry would rather be right than be president." Truman's response was "I'd rather be anything than be president."

Dwight D. Eisenhower

Dwight D. Eisenhower spent his youth known as "Little Ike." He never realized that this nickname would someday appear on posters and presidential campaign buttons during the 1952 presidential campaign. "I Like Ike" is still remembered as a rally call to the nation to elevate this five-star general, with a lifelong military background, as the leader of this country.

U.S. Army

Born in Denison, TX, on October 14, 1890, Dwight was born in a rented room near the railroad tracks to David and Ida Eisenhower. The Eisenhower family moved shortly after Dwight's birth to Abilene, KS. The third of seven sons, Dwight grew up in a relatively poor family. The Eisenhower boys were teased by other children for having to wear hand-me-down clothes and sometimes even their mother's shoes. The brothers were quick to settle a score with their fists, standing up for one another.

All of the boys worked part-time jobs when not in school, and each boy had a garden plot to raise vegetables. Having no daughters, some of the sons, including Dwight, were assigned domestic chores like cooking and sewing.

Although money was lacking, the Eisenhowers were a very close-knit family, and the qualities of a happy and devoted family life were plentiful. They had family prayer daily and weekly Bible study. The boys learned Biblical chapters and verses at an early age. Dwight grew up with a strong work ethic and a respect for handling money wisely.

Education was not highly valued in the late 1800s, but the Eisenhowers insisted on providing good educations for their children. Dwight attended Abilene High School in 1909 where he was a mediocre student who loved reading, history and plane geometry.

Without the money to attend college, Dwight applied for entrance to West Point Military Academy and was accepted in 1911. It is written that his mother, a deeply religious pacifist, wept when her son left for the academy. Although Dwight was an average student, his hard work and discipline made the pressures of West Point easier for him.

Cadet Eisenhower was known as a prankster with a fondness for playing cards and

Artist Concept:

Eisenhower is portrayed as the supreme allied commander on the eve of the Normandy Invasion. One foot stands on England, straddling the English Channel, and one foot stands on Europe, depicting a significant time in the history of the free world.

Sculptor: Lee Leuning | Benefactors: Arthur and Sarah Ludwick

smoking. He received demerits in his senior year for ignoring a warning that he refrain from whirling his dance partner vigorously around the ballroom. During one of his escapades, Dwight was caught making trouble by a senior classmate and was instructed to report to the upper classmate's room for punishment. He was told to appear in his full dress coat, which was a waistcoat with tails. Eisenhower followed these instructions to the letter. He appeared at the senior cadet's door in his dress waistcoat . . . and nothing else! He later wrote, "I enjoyed life at the academy . . . had a good time with my pals and was far from disturbed by an additional demerit or two."

Upon graduation from the academy in 1915, Eisenhower was commissioned as a second lieutenant at the Infantry Regimental Headquarters in San Antonio, TX. One day in October, 1915, he met Mamie Geneva Doud, who was a 19-year-old girl visiting friends on the base. She drew his attention instantly. He recalled her as "a vivacious and attractive

Of Note: **Eisenhower with Normandy map.**

girl, smaller than average, saucy in the look about her face and in her whole attitude." On St. Valentine's Day in 1916 he gave her a miniature of his West Point class ring to seal a formal engagement. They were married at the Doud home in Denver on July 1, 1916. Mamie was raised in a very privileged background, having no domestic skills, so Dwight was responsible for cooking all family meals. When Mamie became pregnant with their first son, Doud Dwight, it was Ike who altered her dresses to accommodate her pregnancy.

The United States entered World War I in April, 1917. Eisenhower had applied for a transfer to Europe, but he was assigned to Camp Colt in Gettysburg, PA, to train officers who were to go overseas.

In December, 1920, Ike and Mamie's three-year-old son died of scarlet fever. Their first child's death affected them both very deeply. For the rest of his life, Ike sent Mamie roses every year on Doud's birthday.

In January, 1922, Eisenhower was transferred to the Panama Canal. During their assignment there, Mamie gave birth to their second son, John. In 1924, Eisenhower was sent to the Army War College and General Staff School where the finest officers and future commanders received special training. In 1926, Eisenhower graduated at the top of his class. Again, his childhood discipline had served him well.

General Douglas MacArthur became army chief of staff in 1930 and made Major Eisenhower his aide in 1932. In June 1941, Ike was assigned to organize and conduct the largest peace-time training exercise in American history. The exercise was a great success, and Eisenhower was promoted to brigadier general in September 1941.

A few days after the bombing of Pearl Harbor, Eisenhower received a call from General George Marshall, the army chief of staff in Washington, D. C. The order was very clear: "Hop a plane and get here right away." In December 1943, President Franklin Roosevelt named Eisenhower the supreme allied commander of the forces in Europe. After the bombing of

Dwight D. Eisenhower

Hiroshima and Nagasaki, the war ended on September 2, 1945. Eisenhower was a five-star general by that time and emerged from the war a world hero.

After World War II, Eisenhower served first as the army chief of staff and then as commander of the North Atlantic Treaty Organization (NATO) in 1951 at the request of President Harry Truman. While commanding NATO forces in 1952, Ike was courted as a presidential candidate. It was not Eisenhower's wish to enter the political arena, but he overcame his misgivings and announced his candidacy. Running on the Republican ticket, he defeated Democratic candidate Adlai Stevenson.

When President Eisenhower took office on January 20, 1953, he was the first Republican in office in 20 years. He fought off increases in Social Security. Congress passed Eisenhower's Federal Aid Highway act, creating 41,000 miles of modern interstate highways. In 1955, he suffered his first of many subsequent heart attacks.

Eisenhower's negotiations with the communist North Koreans and China led to an armistice that was signed on July 27, 1953, and Eisenhower was credited with the ending of the unpopular Korean War. He easily won a second presidential term, running against Stevenson again. Eisenhower received 457 electoral votes to Stevenson's 73, an overwhelming testimony to this national hero.

Among the president's hobbies of fly-fishing and painting, was his passion for golf. Some columnists joked that he was more interested in his handicap than foreign affairs. Actually, Ike's obsession with the sport was a dodge. His drives and putts held the attention of the media while he worked quietly behind the scenes to deal with controversial issues, using his "hidden hand" to guide policy while allowing his subordinates to take any credit, as well as the political heat.

Eisenhower left the White House in 1961 at the age of 70. It was the first time since he left Abilene for West Point that he was not in public service. Eisenhower did not know how to dial a telephone and did not have a driver's license. Ike and Mamie quietly returned to their home in Gettysburg. It is documented that Mamie and her husband moved 28 times before their retirement. Polls taken at the time showed Eisenhower as the most respected and admired man in the country.

Although Eisenhower quit his four-pack-a-day smoking habit in 1949, he still lived with the consequences. In November 1965, Ike had another heart attack. Mamie was so distressed over the president's health that she took it upon herself to personally answer the thousands of well wishes from the public. Each attack weakened him more, and, on March 28, 1969, he ordered the doctors and nurses attending him to lower the shades and pull him up to a sitting position in bed. Then, holding Mamie's hand, 78-year-old Eisenhower looked at his son, John, and grandson, David, and softly issued his final order: "I want to go; God take me." With these words, he died.

Very few campaign slogans have withstood the passage of time, but "I Like Ike" was more than a slogan. It was a declaration of respect for a man who brought dedication to his country and integrity to the office of the presidency.

John F. Kennedy

"Ask not what your country can do for you—ask what you can do for your country." At the time President John Fitzgerald Kennedy made this statement in his inaugural address, little did he know that he would pay the ultimate sacrifice by giving his life for his country.

John F. Kennedy was one of nine children born to Joseph and Rose Kennedy. The children enjoyed a privileged childhood of elite private schools, sailboats, servants and summer homes. Joe was a driving force in all his children's lives, creating one of the strongest political dynasties in American history. He was a very wealthy man, using his resources to pave the way for the political futures of four of his sons.

Born on May 29, 1917, John (Jack) was a very frail and sickly child. He was plagued by many illnesses throughout his life. Some were life threatening. Born with one leg shorter than the other, his back problems began at an early age and affected his health severely. Jack's mother, Rose, nursed him through whooping cough, bronchitis, appendicitis, asthma, measles, scarlet fever, chicken pox and liver disease. Joe, Sr., emphasized the need for all his children to succeed by telling them, "We don't want any losers around here. In this family, we only want winners."

What young Jack lacked in physical strength, he made up in personality. John charmed his way out of most situations. Although John's teachers took a liking to him as a pleasant child, he was not an exceptional student. Even when John wrote a "splendid composition," his teacher commented on his horrendous spelling.

While attending Harvard University, John began to show signs of ambition and became more interested in his studies. For his senior thesis, John wrote a paper on "Why England Slept," which was about Great Britain's lack of preparedness for World War II. His father used his contacts with the publishing industry to have the paper published as a book, and it became a best seller. Kennedy was becoming a man to be noticed.

Both Kennedy sons, Joe and John, wanted to enlist in the military. Joe was accepted into

Artist Concept:

Kennedy is shown handing a toy plane to his son, John Jr. This moment in time takes place at the White House after the president is winding down after a cabinet meeting.

Sculptor: John Lopez | Benefactor: The Family of Padiju Merali

the Naval Aviation Cadet Program. When Jack attempted to enlist, he failed the physical for the Army Officers' Candidate School. Only when his father used his political influence with the U. S. Navy was Jack accepted and placed in naval intelligence.

In December 1941, when the Japanese bombed Pearl Harbor, Jack trained with PT boats. Lt. Kennedy was assigned to the South Pacific, commanding PT-109 and a crew of 12. On August 2, 1943, a Japanese destroyer struck Kennedy's boat. Towing a badly burned crew mate by a life-jacket strap clenched in his teeth, Kennedy led the crew's ten survivors on a three-mile swim to refuge on a tiny island. The crew hid from the enemy until Kennedy managed to summon help. Credited with saving his crew, Kennedy was awarded the U. S. Navy and Marine Corps Medal for Valor and a Purple Heart for injuries he sustained. When asked how he became a hero in the war, he replied, "It was involuntary—they sank my boat." Continuing problems with his back and a failed spinal surgery led to John's discharge from the navy.

Of Note: **Kennedy with John Jr.'s toy plane.**

In 1945, Jack began writing for the Hearst family newspapers after leaving the military. In August of that year, Jack again took seriously ill and was diagnosed with Addison's disease. Plagued with Addison's and a spinal condition that had him in constant pain, 28-year-old Kennedy knew that he would have to find the strength to accelerate his political ambitions. He once told a reporter, "My father wanted his eldest son in politics. 'Wanted' isn't the right word, he demanded it.'" He got his start in April 1946 when he was elected to Congress, representing the state of Massachusetts. He then went on to re-election in 1948 and 1950.

During a dinner party in Washington, D. C., Kennedy met an attractive young socialite named Jacqueline Bouvier. Jackie came from a high-society background and was known as much for her intelligence as her beauty. After a sporadic courtship and Jack's election to the Senate in 1952, John Fitzgerald Kennedy and Jacqueline Bouvier were married on September 12, 1953.

Senator Kennedy continued to suffer from back pain. He went on to have an unsuccessful back surgery that nearly took his life. During his recovery, Kennedy wrote his second best seller, *Profiles in Courage*, a book that went on to win a Pulitzer Prize. Over his lifetime, Kennedy received the last rites of the Catholic Church four times.

In 1956, Jackie Kennedy gave birth to a stillborn baby girl named Arabella. The death of their daughter put a strain on their marriage. However, the birth of Caroline Bouvier Kennedy on November 27, 1957, pulled them together. On November 25, 1960, John Fitzgerald Kennedy, Jr., was born. In 1963, the Kennedy's had a second son named Patrick Bouvier Kennedy who died three days after his birth

On January 2, 1960, Kennedy announced his candidacy for president. Early in the campaign, Kennedy's opponent for the nomination, Minnesota Senator Hubert Humphrey, complained that competing against the wealthy Kennedys was like being a simple shopkeeper running against a national chain. Calling on his Irish wit, Kennedy composed an imaginary telegram from his father stating, "Dear Jack. Don't buy one vote more than necessary. I'll be damned if I'll pay for a landslide." Kennedy easily won the nomination on the first ballot and went on to win the 1960 presidential race over Richard Nixon by the narrowest margin of any presidential election in the century. At 43, he was the first Roman Catholic and youngest president ever elected.

Kennedy's presidency was notable for his strong stand on civil rights, the inception of the space program (NASA) and the creation of the Peace Corps. He successfully handled the Cuban missile crisis and failed the Bay of Pigs insurgence. Kennedy was once quoted as saying, "We stand today at the edge of a new frontier—the frontier of the 1960s—a frontier of unknown opportunities and perils—a frontier of unfulfilled hopes and threats."

As Kennedy was preparing to run for his second term as president, he and Jackie traveled to Dallas, TX, with Vice-President Lyndon Johnson and Lady Bird Johnson. During a motorcade on November 22, 1963, while driving through the streets of downtown Dallas in an open convertible, shots rang out, striking the president. He was pronounced dead at the Parkland Hospital. Hours later, Johnson was sworn in as president in a somber ceremony aboard Air Force One with Jacqueline in attendance.

Fifty years after his assassination, people have varying opinions and memories regarding Kennedy's presidency. The fact remains that people remember more about the days of "Camelot" and the Kennedys than any other political family of the century, and John Fitzgerald Kennedy will always be revered for "what he gave for his country."

JFK and Jackie seconds before his assassination.

Lyndon B. Johnson

Lyndon Baines Johnson learned firsthand that the vice presidency was only a heartbeat away from the presidency when he took the presidential oath of office after the assassination of President John F. Kennedy on November 22, 1963.

White House Press Office

Lyndon was born August 27, 1908, in the Pedernales Valley of central Texas. Born to Sam Ealy and Rebekah Johnson, Lyndon was the eldest of five children and his mother's favorite.

Sam Ealy was a member of the Texas state legislature while struggling to run his ranch in the Pedernales Valley. Sam made fortunes and lost them, putting his family in both wealth and want. Lyndon often spoke of his poor beginnings, showing visitors a ramshackle house where he claimed he was born. In fact, this house was about a mile from the comfortable home of his birth.

Young Lyndon and his siblings had plenty of chores at the ranch, although Lyndon delegated jobs rather than doing the work himself. The small Johnson City High School offered classes only through the 11th grade, so Lyndon was a high school graduate at the age of 15 and already over six-feet tall.

All through his adolescent years, Lyndon was prone to exaggeration and rebellion. Upon high school graduation, he headed to California to find work, but times were hard, and he was only able to find menial jobs. To others, he claimed that he was weak, near starvation and hitchhiked all the way back to Texas. In fact, a friend drove him home. His brother, Sam Houston Johnson, said, "Lyndon often remembered things as being worse than they were."

Borrowing money and doing odd jobs on campus, Johnson was able to enter Southwest Texas State Teachers College in 1927 and graduated two years later with a teaching degree. After a short term of teaching English to Mexican-American children, he returned to Southwest Texas State University to complete his college education.

In 1931, a newly elected congressman from Texas, Richard Kleberg, offered Johnson a job as his personal secretary. Lyndon took on the position with the energy for which he

Artist Concept:

This statue depicts Johnson in "the Johnson treatment" pose. He is shown here with a forward thrust of his body that tended to intimidate those around him. The books on the desk are Machiavelli's The Prince *and* The Great Society. *Engraved on the back of the desk is a map of Vietnam.*

Sculptor: James Michael Maher | Benefactor: Pat Hall (in honor of three classmates killed in Vietnam)

became famous. Working long hours for an often absentee congressman, Johnson soon learned the ins and outs of Congress and became a force to be reckoned with.

During the Great Depression, President Franklin Roosevelt was elected on promises to help unemployed Americans. Roosevelt met and developed an immediate liking to Johnson. On June 26, 1935, Roosevelt established the National Youth Administration (NYA) to provide employment for the country's unemployed young people and appointed Johnson as director. At 27, Johnson was the youngest NYA state director in the nation.

In September of 1934, Lyndon met Claudia Alta Taylor, who was the daughter of a wealthy Texas landowner and known as "Lady Bird." On their first date, he proposed marriage, and within seven weeks, the couple married and eventually had two daughters—Lynda Byrd and Luci Baines. Claudia was a perfect balance for him. She was charming and refined, where he was raw and boisterous. As an example, Johnson was later declared the best dancer in the White House since Washington.

Of Note: **LBJ with a memorial to fallen Vietnam veterans.**

In February 1937, the U. S. congressman from Johnson's Texas district died, and he was urged to run for the vacated congressional seat. On April 10, Johnson won the election with twice as many votes as his closest rival. At the age of 28, Johnson was elected to the U. S. House of Representatives. His relationship with Roosevelt continued to flourish, and Johnson, only a freshman congressman from Texas, had a very powerful friend. In later years, Johnson was heard referring to FDR as a "second daddy."

When the Japanese bombed Pearl Harbor on December 7, 1941, Congressman Johnson entered the navy, rising to the rank of lieutenant commander and winning a Silver Star.

By 1948, Johnson had served five terms in the House. Urged by his fellow Texans to seek a seat in the Senate, Johnson campaigned in his usual flamboyant style. Using a helicopter to cover the vast Texas area, people came to recognize Johnson by his arrival in the "Johnson City Flying Windmill." He won the election by a total of 87 votes out of nearly a million cast.

Senator Johnson arrived on the floor of the U. S. Senate running. He knew that getting legislation passed was a process of "wheeling and dealing." His energetic style and 6'3" frame made a formidable presence, and Johnson's way of convincing others with unyielding persuasion soon became known as the "Johnson Treatment." He was known to poke the listener in the chest and stand very close to intimidate them. Vice-President Hubert Humphrey once showed a reporter the cuts and bruises on his shins inflicted under the table by an impatient president. Few were able to defy Johnson when he made up his mind to do something.

He won a second term in the Senate in 1954 under the presidency of Dwight Eisenhower. In 1955, he became the Senate majority leader. Although Eisenhower suggested that America adopt a minimum wage law, many feel that it was Johnson's leadership that established the first minimum wage law of $1 per hour.

Lyndon B. Johnson

Senator Johnson suffered a life-threatening heart attack on July 2, 1955. Returning to his office only six months later, he began working tirelessly for civil rights to guarantee black citizens the right to register to vote. He also became the youngest Senate majority leader.

In the 1960 presidential race, Johnson had been considered a strong candidate for the Democratic nominee, but John F. Kennedy won the nomination on the first ballot. Knowing that Johnson was well liked in the southern states, Kennedy chose Johnson as his running mate, and Kennedy went on to win the 1960 presidential race. It is said that Johnson found being second-in-command tedious after having had such an energetic schedule as the Senate majority leader. However, on November 22, 1963, all of that changed.

During a trip to Johnson's home state of Texas, a motorcade driving through Dallas came under fire, and President John F. Kennedy was shot. As the hospital announced the death of the president, Johnson, accompanied by Lady Bird Johnson and Jacqueline Kennedy, boarded Air Force One where Johnson was administered the presidential oath of office.

During the early months of his presidency, Johnson was able to use the "Johnson Treatment" to achieve success on many of the issues before the country at that time due to his past experience in the House and the Senate. He was able to enact the Civil Rights Act and was able to get laws passed that resulted in the Neighborhood Youth Corps, Head Start, Job Corps, Vista and Medicare.

One of the most difficult challenges that faced Johnson was the growing Vietnam War during the next presidential race. Republican Senator Barry Goldwater ran against Johnson, calling for a new direction in Vietnam.

When the election day of November 4, 1964, arrived, Johnson won a smashing victory, receiving 43 million votes to Goldwater's 27 million. During his second term, the Vietnam War escalated dramatically. Johnson was forced to deal with a seemingly unwinnable war, racial riots that were taking over the streets of the country and violent anti-war demonstrations. His second term saw the assassinations of Martin Luther King, Jr., and Robert F. Kennedy.

In 1968, as the presidential election neared, Johnson appeared on national television to declare that he would not run for another term. He chose to leave public life and return to his ranch in the Perdernales Valley.

Johnson died of a heart attack on the afternoon of January 22, 1973, in the bedroom of his beloved ranch. Five days after his death, the United States and North Vietnam signed a peace treaty, and a cease-fire was declared.

Johnson biographers give very different analyses of Johnson's life and presidency. He was known as a bully, egotist, manipulator and liar—as well as a brilliant man who was passionate about the rights of all men regardless of race, religion, social status or economics. Some say he was a brilliant politician, while some saw him as a shifty wheeler-and-dealer. In the opinion of most historians, however, President Lyndon Johnson will clearly be ranked in the top quarter of their lists.

Richard Nixon

A little known fact about Richard Milhous Nixon is that while attending Duke University he once broke into a professor's office to look at the grade sheets because he was worried about his grades. As it turns out, he was relieved to find out he was third in his class. He ended up graduating from Duke with honors. He wasn't so lucky the next time paranoia got the best of him.

Richard Nixon once psychoanalyzed himself to his aid, Ken Clawson. He said, "What starts the process really are laughs and slights and snubs when you are a kid . . . but if you are reasonably intelligent and if your anger is deep enough and strong enough you learn that you can change those attitudes by excellence [and] personal gut performances, while those who have everything are sitting on their fat butts."

Richard was born on January 9, 1913, in Yorba Linda, CA, the second son of Hannah and Frank Nixon, who were Quakers and poor citrus farmers. They lived in a house that Richard's father built without indoor plumbing that. In 1918, when Hannah gave birth to her fourth son, Arthur, all four boys shared a small upstairs bedroom. Richard had close relationships with his brothers, especially one named "Harold." Unfortunately, both Harold and Arthur died when Richard was young, and these tragedies affected Nixon the rest of his life,

When Richard entered school, his classmates called him "Gloomy Gus." His first teacher said, "He was a very solemn child and rarely smiled or laughed." On the other hand, Richard loved to read, and the teacher recalled that "He absorbed knowledge of any kind like a blotter." By the age of six, he was discussing current affairs with his father.

At the age of nine, Richard's family moved to the Quaker community of Whittier where they ran a grocery store and gas station. Young Richard woke up at 4:00 a.m. each morning to travel with his father to buy fresh vegetables. Despite this grueling schedule, Nixon was a top student but not very popular. In fact, he was picked on quite a bit. Nixon's way of getting back at the students was not by revenge but by succeeding.

Both Harvard and Yale Universities approached Nixon, offering him full scholarships. However, he didn't have the money necessary to pay for the living expenses to attend either university. So, he chose to live at home and attend a much smaller one called Whittier

Artist Concept:

This statue depicts Nixon during delicate negotiations with China regarding trade with the Western world. He is posed in a Chinese-style chair with his hands in a power posture negotiating with Mao Tse-Tun (Zedong).

Sculptor: Edward E. Hlavka | Benefactors: Arthur and Sarah Ludwick, Dr. Edward and Peg Seljeskog

College. Nixon was an active student while still helping in the family business. He continued to receive excellent grades and even made the freshman football team. Nixon's football coach had no tolerance for losing and would say, "Show me a good loser and I'll show you a loser." This attitude of winning at all costs stayed with Nixon throughout his political life.

He graduated from Whittier College in 1934, ranking second in his graduating class. Then he read that Duke University was offering scholarships for their law school. He applied and was accepted. The president of Whittier College said the following in recommending Nixon to Duke: "I cannot recommend him too highly because I believe that Nixon will become one of America's important, if not greatest, leaders."

After graduating from Duke in mid-1937 and passing the bar exam, he took a position with a Whittier law firm. A year later, while auditioning for a play at a local theatre, Nixon met a pretty school teacher named Thelma Catherine Ryan, who was nicknamed "Pat." It was love at first sight. Nixon told her, "I think we should go out because I am going to marry you some day." Although he proposed on their first date, it took two years for Pat to accept his offer of marriage.

They married on June 21, 1940, and had two girls named Trisha and Julie in 1946 and 1948, respectively. Shortly after they were married, Nixon took a job as a lawyer in Washington, D. C., in the Office of Price Administration (OPA). He was to start his new position in January 1942. However, on December 7, 1941, the Japanese bombed Pearl Harbor, and Nixon enlisted in the navy and served in the South Pacific. Upon arriving back in the states in 1944, Nixon received a letter from the Republican committee, asking him to run for Congress in the 1946 election. Nixon accepted the offer and moved back to California to begin his campaign.

At that time, Americans feared that communism would invade U. S. shores. Many Republicans accused Democrats of having communist views. Nixon took this approach during the 1946 campaign, inferring that his opponent had accepted support from a communist political group. Nixon did win the election but, years later, admitted that he knew his opponent had no communist affiliations saying, "but I had to win. That's the thing you don't understand. The important thing is to win."

In 1947, Nixon arrived in Washington, D. C., and befriended another young congressman from Massachusetts named John F. Kennedy. Although from different parties, they had mutual respect for each other. One historian described the relationship this way, " . . . The only way I can describe it is that Richard Nixon was the smart kid in the class, and Kennedy was the cool kid in the class."

Nixon served on the House Committee on Un-American Activities, which was formed to find people or groups whose ideas threatened the security of the United States. In 1948, Nixon won the Senate seat by a landslide after inferring, once again, that his Democractic opponent was a communist sympathizer.

In the 1952 presidential campaign, General Dwight Eisenhower was the Republican candidate, running against Adlai Stevenson. Eisenhower was a 62-year-old moderate

Republican who needed a younger, more conservative running mate. At 39, Nixon was the perfect match. In November, the Eisenhower/Nixon ticket won by a landslide, receiving 442 electoral votes over Stephenson's 89 votes.

Eisenhower and Nixon easily won a second term over Stevenson as well, in 1956, by a larger margin. In the 1960 election, Nixon was the Republican's nominee for president, and Nixon's friend, John Kennedy, was the Democratic candidate. Nixon ended up losing to Kennedy in one of the closest elections in U. S. history. Many believe that the televised debate between Nixon and Kennedy showed the contrast between the pale, sweaty and ill Nixon and the bronze, poised and robust Kennedy.

Following President Kennedy's assassination in 1963 and the subsequent presidency of Lyndon Johnson, Nixon again entered the presidential race in 1969. Johnson chose not to run again due to his frustrations over the Vietnam War. Nixon easily won his party's nomination and the presidential election by less than one percent of the popular vote.

During his presidency, Nixon gradually began to withdraw troops from Vietnam. However, the country felt this was too little, too late, and protests began erupting throughout the campuses of America. In 1971, secret documents discussing the United States involvement in Vietnam (The Pentagon Papers) were released to the American public. These documents revealed unprecedented misconduct at the highest level and the extent of dirty politics being practiced. The release of these papers was an embarrassment to Nixon.

One of the successes of Nixon's presidency was making an historic trip to China, later described as a "week that changed the world." His public popularity easily gave him the opportunity to run for a second term. Running against South Dakota Senator George McGovern, Nixon and running mate, Spiro Agnew, won the largest victory of any president in the history of the Electoral College, capturing 49 states. However, troubles began soon after the election when Agnew resigned over accusations of bribery and tax evasion. Nixon then nominated Gerald R. Ford to replace Agnew.

In 1972, it was learned that Nixon had been involved with authorizing illegal wiretaps and a burglary of the Democratic Party headquarters at the Watergate Hotel. This indicated that Nixon's campaign committee and White House aides had been engaged in covert and illegal activities to sabotage the other side. Due to the Senate Watergate Committee hearings, it became apparent that Nixon would soon be impeached. Choosing to leave office on his own terms, Nixon went on national television to announce his resignation. Ford assumed the presidency on August 9, 1974, and one month later, Ford gave him a "full, free and absolute pardon." On April 18, 1994, Nixon suffered a stroke and died four days later.

Due to the Watergate scandal, Nixon may generate a negative emotional response from most. Herb Stein, Nixon's chief economic advisor, summed it up by saying, "I think he should be remembered as a man who achieved a great deal, both in his personal life and in his career as president, but who made some bad mistakes and who, in the end, paid for those mistakes. If you were to take away Watergate, he would be remembered as a very good president. I think he was a very good, but a flawed, president."

Gerald Ford

Gerald R. Ford had the dubious distinction of becoming the first man to occupy the White House without being elected either president or vice president. He also bore the unique experience of surviving two assassination attempts within one month in September 1975.

White House

Born in Omaha, NE, on July 14, 1913, he was christened Leslie Lynch King, Jr. Unfortunately, his father was an alcoholic and a wife beater, and his parents divorced when he was two. Soon, his mother remarried. He then took the name of his stepfather, Gerald Rudolph Ford. Jerry did not know that he was adopted, as was the custom in the 1920s. So, it was a shock for 17-year-old Jerry when his birth father walked into the restaurant he was working at in Grand Rapids at the time and introduced himself. After a brief, awkward lunch, King slipped the boy $25 and drove off in a shiny new Lincoln. King visited him again while Ford was attending Yale Law School. Ford bitterly resented King as a carefree man of wealth, indifferent to his first-born son. Gerald, Jr., later described his stepfather as a man whose honesty and integrity made the strongest impression on his life.

Regardless of his birth father's abandonment, Jerry's childhood was a happy one. He loved sports, fishing and outdoor activities. School and church activities were very important to him as well. His parents were strict but loving disciplinarians, and there were rules in the household that were strongly enforced. Occasionally, he was caught playing penny-ante poker and was strictly punished. However, he was basically a good, obedient son.

Jerry had one unique characteristic that stayed with him throughout his life. When he was sitting down, he used his left hand, and when he stood, he used his right hand. Therefore, he wrote left-handed and threw a football right-handed. Ford believed this trait was quite natural. The one vice that Ford did admit to was an eight-bowl-a-day pipe habit with Prince Albert tobacco.

Ford was educated in Grand Rapids, MI. In high school, he made the National Honor

Artist Concept:

Ford is shown here with his golden retriever, Liberty, who frequently shared the Oval Office with the president.

Sculptor: John Michael Maher | Benefactors: The Rypkema Family of Dodgetown and an Anonymous donor from Nebraska

Society and ranked in the top five percent of his class. After graduation, he attended the University of Michigan on a football scholarship where he studied economics and political science, graduating in the top 25 percent of his class. Football was a very important part of his college experience, having played on two national championship teams. After graduation, both the Detroit Lions and the Green Bay Packers professional football teams offered Ford a contract. He turned them both down, choosing to enter law school instead. In later years, Jerry said that playing football taught him how to be a team player—a lesson that would serve him well the rest of his life.

He attended Yale University and was also hired as an assistant football coach in 1935 at $2,400 a year. Winning admission to Yale Law School proved difficult, but Ford persisted and eventually was accepted on a trial basis in 1938, graduating in the top third of his class and earning a law degree in 1941. He went on to practice law in Grand Rapids, MI. During his time at Yale, he was also a fashion model for *Look* and *Cosmopolitan* magazines.

When World War II broke out, Ford enlisted in the navy as an aviation operations officer and saw action aboard the Monterey in the South Pacific, winning ten battle stars for his service. He was discharged four years later as a lieutenant commander. His wartime experiences convinced him that America should never again allow its military defenses to weaken. He also recognized the importance of America needing strong allies to fend off the growing threat of communism.

Ford was basically a very shy person with a quiet social life. Through a mutual friend, he met divorcee Elizabeth (Betty) Bloomer, a professional dancer with the famous Martha Graham concert group. They went on to marry on October 15, 1948, while Ford was campaigning for election as the fifth congressional district representative. On their wedding day, Ford had attended a rally just before the ceremony and traipsed down the aisle in muddy shoes. On their unusual honeymoon, the newlyweds drove to Ann Arbor for the Michigan/Northwestern football game and went on to hear Thomas Dewey, the Republican presidential nominee, address an outdoor rally that evening. Ford soon won his own election, beginning his 25-year career in Congress.

Arriving in Washington, Ford became dedicated to America retaining its position of world leadership. He fought hard for a strong national defense budget and a powerful American military presence around the world. Ford was assigned an office next to Democrat John F. Kennedy from Massachusetts. Richard Nixon, a representative from California, occupied an office upstairs. Having all served in the navy during World War II, they developed a close friendship.

When Kennedy won the 1960 presidential election, members of both parties chose Ford to be the highest-ranking Republican on the defense subcommittee, which controlled the largest portion of the national budget. Upon the assassination of his close friend, Kennedy, Ford was appointed to the Warren Commission to investigate the Kennedy murder.

After the election of Nixon to the presidency in 1968, Vietnam, the economy, civil rights issues and international diplomatic problems continued to take a toll on the American

people. In 1973, when Nixon's vice president, Spiro Agnew, was charged with tax evasion and forced to give up the vice presidency, Ford was chosen to replace him. When asked about his personal political philosophy, Ford replied, "Moderate in domestic affairs, conservative in fiscal affairs, and dyed-in-the-wool internationalist in foreign affairs."

On August 8, 1974, in the wake of the Watergate investigation, Nixon resigned as president. One day later, Gerald R. Ford was sworn in as the 38th president of the United States. After only one month in office, Ford issued a pardon to former President Nixon because he thought a trial would divide the country even more deeply. This controversial decision contributed greatly to his political future.

In September 1974, two separate attempts were made on Ford's life—one on September 5 by Lynette "Squeaky" Fromme, who was a follower of mass-murderer Charles Manson, and the second on September 22 by Sara Jane Moore, a political activist and former FBI informant.

Given little time to prepare for the task at hand, Ford served only two-and-a-half years in office. Unable to turn the economy around, establish international relationships or heal the nation over the Watergate scandal, Ford was defeated by Jimmy Carter in 1976. After the pardon of Nixon, Ford later wrote, "I began to wonder whether, instead of healing the wounds, my decision had only rubbed salt in them."

In his retirement years, Ford continued his work as a diplomat for the U. S. in the international arena. He and his wife worked tirelessly with the Betty Ford Center, a treatment center for the chemically dependent, which she founded. President Bill Clinton awarded 86-year-old Ford the Presidential Medal of Freedom in August 1999 in honor of his public service in binding the nation together after "the nightmare" of Watergate. Ford died at his Rancho Mirage, CA, home on December 26, 2006.

President Nixon and First Lady Pat Nixon with Betty and Gerald Ford after Nixon nominated Ford vice president in 1973.

Jimmy Carter

"I'm Jimmy Carter, and I'm going to be your next president," said an unknown political outsider who began his campaign by walking the streets of America and shaking hands with the common man. Amazingly, this is how Jimmy's campaign started, and it worked.

Department of Defense

James Earl Carter, Jr., was born on October 1, 1924, in Plains, GA, to Earl and "Miz" Lillian Carter. He was the first American president born in a hospital. However, he was then taken home to a house lacking indoor plumbing and electricity.

Jimmy spent his childhood years working the fields of his father's peanut farm. His father was a difficult taskmaster, beginning each work day for the entire family at 4:00 a.m. Even as a small child, Jimmy was expected to put in a full day's work in the field or suffer the consequences of being ". . . licked with a switch" from a peach tree. He learned very early about the importance of reaping the rewards of hard work.

Earl Carter eventually expanded his farm to 4,000 acres, thanks to his family's hard work and the hard work of 200 sharecroppers. He treated these people no better and no worse than any other white Georgia farmer of the 1920s, although he did not allow anyone with dark skin into his house. "Miz" Lillian set a different moral example for her son by crossing the strict lines of segregation. A nurse, she counseled poor African-American women on matters of health care. Often in disagreement with her husband, Lillian insisted on allowing African-Americans to visit the house, while Earl stormed out when the visitors arrived.

At the age of five, Jimmy began gathering peanuts from his father's fields, boiling them overnight and selling them for five cents a bag the next day. When he was ten years old, he loaded produce from the family farm and sold it to the local townspeople. By the age of 13, he had saved enough money to buy five houses in and around Plains at rock-bottom prices during the Great Depression, renting these houses out to local residents and family members.

Artist Concept:

Carter is portrayed here as a man of the people, not one who enjoys a lot of formality. He is shown walking down Pennsylvania Avenue in a stylish plaid polyester suit. To accentuate his casual demeanor, his jacket is off and his tie is flying in the wind. Notice the peanut on the plaque.

Sculptor: John Lopez | Benefactors: Ray Godfrey, Don Herrmann, Jim and Julia Meier, Don and Joan Perdue

Young Carter attended school in Plains. His mother constantly encouraged him to read, allowing him to bring books to the dinner table. Jimmy once had a teacher who saw something in her student that warranted exposing him to literature, music and art. Challenged to read *War and Peace*, he took on the task of reading the 1,400-page classic because he thought it was a book about cowboys and Indians. To this day, it's still his favorite book. Jimmy was not only the first member of the Carter family to graduate high school, but he was also his class's valedictorian.

At 14, Jimmy dreamed that he would escape Plains by attending the United States Naval Academy at Annapolis, MD. Worried that the physical tests disallowed flat feet, he spent hours rolling his feet over Coke bottles to strengthen his weakened arches.

To support his son's commitment to attend Annapolis, Earl did everything he could to garner the influence needed for his son's appointment. Flat feet weren't a problem. After graduating from the academy in the top ten percent of his class, Carter was personally selected by Admiral Hyman Rickover to serve with both the Atlantic and Pacific fleets as a lieutenant, working under the admiral to develop the nuclear submarine program. Admiral Rickover served as an example of a perfectionist leader and profoundly influenced Carter the rest of his life.

Prior to his last year at Annapolis, 20-year-old Midshipman Carter met 17-year-old Rosalynn Smith, who was a friend of his sister's. In July 1946, Carter married Rosalynn. When Earl Carter died of cancer in 1953, the family peanut farm and his mother's livelihood were in jeopardy. Despite his rapid move up the military ranks, Carter resigned from the navy and returned to the family business as a progressive landowner and prosperous businessman. Carter became a deacon and Sunday School teacher before he began his political career in state politics in 1962. When he lost his first bid for governor of Georgia in 1966, he suffered a deep depression. Although he had been only a superficial Christian most of his life, he sought the counsel of his evangelistic sister, Ruth Carter Stapleton. The result was a religious experience that lifted his depression and gave a new shape to his public life.

In December 1974, he declared his candidacy for president. Carter won the 1976 Democratic Party's presidential nomination on the first ballot with running mate Senator Walter Mondale, who was a liberal from Minnesota.

Carter's presidency required all the traits of a statesman, diplomat, economist and peacemaker. The nation faced high unemployment, energy problems, threats of nuclear war and high oil prices that could stagger the American economy. In addition, there was unrest in the Middle East that had potential for great conflict.

In 1977, Carter established the U. S. Department of Energy. This agency was given directive to find new sources of energy to offset the high prices of oil established by the OPEC nations. In 1978, Carter mediated an historic peace agreement (the Camp David Accords) between Israel's Menachem Began and Egypt's Anwar Sadat. Also that year, Carter initiated the ratification of a treaty with Panama, which gave that country control of the Panama Canal in the year 2000. In addition, Carter initiated dialogue between the U. S. and the People's Republic of China. As a result, diplomatic relations were established on January 1, 1979. He also formulated plans for SALT II talks, which would limit nuclear weapons by U. S. and the Soviet Union. President Carter was also a dedicated defender of human rights with a deep commitment to the environment. In fact, he is credited with adding 103 million acres of Alaskan wilderness to the National Parks Service.

Although known as a common man with a common touch, a southern drawl and a wide smile, those who knew Carter saw another side of him. One White House staffer once said, "His insides are made of twisted steel cable." Carter admits, "It's been very difficult for me to compromise when I believe in something deeply."

Despite his efforts toward global peace, Carter was unable to stop the unrest that developed throughout the world. Furthermore, in 1979, 66 Americans were taken hostage in Tehran, and the Soviet Union invaded Afghanistan. The president's commitment to international human rights resulted in his difficult decision to boycott the 1980 Olympics in Moscow over the Soviet Union's aggression in Afghanistan.

As a result of these events, Carter was badly defeated by Republican Ronald Reagan in 1980. On January 21, 1981, as Reagan was being sworn in as the new president, the U. S. hostages were released.

After leaving the White House, the Carters continued to work in public service. Their work with Habitat for Humanity has made an impact on the people of America. In October 2002, Carter was awarded the Nobel Peace Prize for his peacemaking efforts between Egypt and Israel and his lifelong commitment to humanity and diplomacy. Keeping his sense of humor after a difficult one-term presidency, Carter was quoted as saying, "My esteem in this country has gone up substantially. It is very nice now, when people wave at me, they use all their fingers."

Inauguration of Jimmy Carter in 1977.

RONALD REAGAN
BORN 1911
FORTIETH PRESIDENT
OF THE
UNITED STATES
1981-1989

CHUCK AND BARBARA LEWIS

Ronald Reagan

In commenting on his rise from humble beginnings to president of the United States, Ronald Reagan wrote, "The dreams of people may differ but everyone wants their dreams to come true . . . and America, above all places, gives us the freedom to do that; the freedom to reach out and make our dreams come true."

White House

Ronald Wilson Reagan was born on February 6, 1911, in a five-room rented flat over a bakery in Tampico, Ill. Legend has it that when Ronald's father, Jack, first saw his newborn son, he said, "He looks like a fat little Dutchman. But who knows, he might grow up to be president some day." From that moment on, Reagan was called "Dutch."

Between 1914 and 1920, Jack Reagan moved the family, including Ronald and his older brother, Neil, four times to pursue jobs as a shoe salesman. Both boys worked at part-time jobs to help the family buy things they needed. Until he was in college, Dutch wore Neil's hand-me-down clothes.

Reagan was five years old when his mother, Nelle, taught him to read. She stressed the importance of college to her sons. Dutch began saving his wages from various jobs, knowing the family would not have the money to send him to college. To earn money, he took a summer job at the age of 14, digging house foundations for 35 cents an hour. When the Ringling Brothers Circus came to town, he worked as a roustabout for 25 cents an hour.

For seven summers, Ronald was a lifeguard at Lowell Park. An excellent swimmer, he marked an old park log for every swimmer he saved. When he finally stopped being a lifeguard, he had 77 notches on the log. Although few of those saved by Reagan ever expressed their thanks, one gentlemen tipped Ronald $10 for retrieving his false teeth from the water. When he graduated from high school, he had saved $400 toward his college fund. Despite the poverty of his youth and the stress of dealing with his father's alcoholism, Reagan recalls his childhood as the happiest time of his life.

In 1928, Dutch enrolled at Eureka College. While in high school, Ronald had played

Artist Concept:

The sculptor chose to depict Reagan in western attire because he loved working on his ranch. Upon Reagan's death, a spontaneous public memorial of ribbons, balloons and jelly beans were placed by his statue.

Sculptor: James Michael Mayer | Benefactors: Chuck and Barbara Lien

football, and he convinced the college football coach that he was a good football player and a hard worker. As a result, he was given a scholarship to pay half his tuition, and he washed dishes to pay the second half. As it turns out, Dutch spent more time outside the classroom than he did on his studies.

He was an athlete, cheerleader, member of the student senate, editor of the yearbook and student body president. Reagan graduated in 1932 with a degree in economics and social science. His dream was to be an actor but settled on being a sports announcer. When he became a sportscaster, the games were sent to Reagan over the teletype in Morse code. He then described the action over the radio as if he was watching the game in person.

Reagan's dream of becoming an actor never died. While covering the Chicago Cubs baseball team's spring training in California, Reagan went to Hollywood. A screen test was arranged for him, and Warner Brothers Studios hired him at $200 a week. However, one concern Hollywood executives had was using the name "Dutch." Wanting to keep the family name, Reagan suggested "Ronald." The studio agreed, and so the acting career of Ronald Reagan began.

From 1937 to 1964, Reagan made 53 movies. He usually played the wholesome, all-American hero. In 1938, he met actress Jane Wyman. On January 26, 1940, Reagan and Jane Wyman were married. A year later, daughter, Maureen, was born. In 1945, the Reagans then adopted a four-day-old son named Michael.

During World War II, Reagan took time off from acting to serve with the U. S. Army. After being discharged in 1945, Captain Reagan returned to Hollywood where he became more involved in the political aspects of the movie industry. Some in the movie business were being blacklisted because they were suspected of being communists. At that time, Reagan was the president of the Screen Actors Guild (SAG) and testified before the House Un-American Activities Committee (HUAC), defending the actors on the blacklists even though he was against communism.

Reagan continued his political activism in the film industry, but his wife did not share this interest. In June 1948, the couple divorced. Shortly after his divorce, Ronald met Nancy Davis, a young actress who had come to Reagan because her name had been erroneously put on the blacklist. Nancy Davis Reagan was later quoted as saying that her life "didn't really begin" until she met Ronald Reagan.

Ronald and Nancy were married on March 4, 1952. After making a few films, Nancy retired. In October 1952, a daughter, Patricia, was born and a son, Ronald Prescott Reagan, was born six years later.

During their early marriage, Reagan began working for General Electric as the host of a new television drama series, *General Electric Theater*. When the television series was cancelled, Reagan went on to host the Western series, *Death Valley Days*.

Although Reagan had voted as a Democrat in his youth, he campaigned actively during Richard Nixon's presidential run in 1960, delivering over 200 campaign speeches on Nixon's behalf. He formally joined the Republican Party in 1962. In 1965, members of the

California Republican Party asked Reagan to run for governor of California in 1966. His name recognition, experience in public speaking and handsome appearance made him an ideal candidate. In 1966, 54-year-old Reagan was elected governor of California. In 1970, he was easily voted in for a second term.

In 1968, Reagan tried for the Republican presidential nomination but lost to Nixon. In 1976, Reagan again tried for the presidential nomination, but this time it went to Gerald Ford. In 1980, Reagan finally won the Republican nomination for president and chose George H. W. Bush as a running mate. The Reagan/Bush ticket won 489 electoral votes to incumbent President Jimmy Carter's 49. Being the oldest man to be elected president, 69-year-old Reagan's dream of one day becoming president came true.

In his first inaugural address, Reagan said, "It is time for us to realize that we are too great a nation to limit ourselves to small dreams. We're not, as some would have us believe, doomed to an inevitable decline. I do not believe in a fate that will fall on us no matter what we do. I do believe in a fate that will fall on us if we do nothing . . . "

Reagan had run on a platform of cutting taxes, reducing the size of the federal government, cutting government spending, increasing defense spending, appointing more conservative Supreme Court justices and balancing the federal budget. He surrounded himself with a strong cabinet and advisors to get these things done.

On March 30, 1981, an assassination attempt nearly cost the president his life. The public's sympathy toward an injured president encouraged Congress to pass many of his programs. Following the assassination attempt, the air traffic controllers' strike was resolved, summit meetings with Russia began and economic conditions began to improve, just in time for Reagan to make a bid for a second term.

In 1984, the Reagan/Bush team easily defeated Democratic nominee Walter Mondale. From 1984 to 1988, the economy became sluggish yet again. However, Reagan was successful in foreign affairs, especially with the Soviet Union. Ultimately, relations greatly improved. In a famous speech at Brandenburg Gate in West Germany on June 12, 1987, Reagan boldly challenged, "General Secretary Gorbachev, if you see peace . . . come here to this gate. Mr. Gorbachev, tear down this wall." As a result, the wall between East and West Germany came down in 1989.

Successfully surviving cancer surgery in 1985, Reagan completed his second presidential term. After his departure from the presidency in 1989, Reagan continued public speaking until 1994 when a "Letter to the American People" was published. In that letter, Reagan revealed that he suffered from Alzheimer's. His condition deteriorated profoundly over the years, and his devoted wife, Nancy, remained at his bedside until his death on June 5, 2004.

As is true of every president, Reagan's successes and failures will be decided by history. Some feel he was a strong leader who restored the country's confidence in the nation, while critics stress that he was isolated from the day-to-day workings of government. Regardless, his ability to speak to the American people personally earned him the title, "The Great Communicator."

George H.W.Bush

From the time he was a child and throughout his college years, George Herbert Walker Bush was known as "Poppy." Named after his grandfather, George Herbert Walker, young George Bush was called "Little Pop" and eventually "Poppy." Even through his successful years at Yale, the name stuck.

White House

George was born to a family of privilege on June 12, 1924, in Milton, MA. George, his three brothers and sister grew up in the affluence of Greenwich, CT, and Kennebunkport, ME. George's father, Prescott Bush, Sr., was a partner in a Wall Street investment banking firm. George and his siblings attended Greenwich Country Day School and were driven there by the family chauffeur, Alec. Despite their wealth, the Bush children were raised with strong moral values. Their parents instilled a strong sense of duty and service, and the occasional discipline was dispensed with a squash racquet.

After graduating from Greenwich Country Day School, "Poppy" Bush attended Phillips Academy, an exclusive boarding school in Andover, MA. Rapidly growing to a height of over six-feet tall, he became an excellent athlete and excelled in baseball and soccer. At Christmas time in his last year at the academy, George attended a dance where he met 16-year-old Barbara Pierce, the beautiful daughter of the publisher of *McCall's Magazine*. They began dating and fell in love.

In 1941, during his senior year at the academy, the Japanese bombed Pearl Harbor. In 1942, upon graduation from the academy, Bush chose to delay college and enlisted in the navy on his 18th birthday. He entered aviation training, and Bush received his wings after ten months of intense training, becoming the youngest pilot in naval history to do so. Lieutenant Bush went on to serve heroically during the war, serving as a torpedo bomber pilot on aircraft carriers in the Pacific and conducting 58 combat missions. Once, while flying a mission to bomb an enemy radio site, his plane was shot down over the ocean and was rescued by a submarine. For this heroic mission, he was awarded the Distinguished Flying

Artist Concept:

President Bush's administration was extensively involved in the international arena, so he is standing next to a world globe. It is interesting to note that his statue is across from President John Adams. They are the only two presidents to have sons who also served as president.

Sculptor: Edward E. Hlavka | Benefactors: Don and Joan Perdue

Cross. Bush was then ordered home in December, 1944, and George and Barbara Pierce were married on January 6, 1945.

In the fall of 1945, the newlyweds moved to New Haven, CT, and George entered Yale University. During his time at Yale, their first-born son, the future President George Walker Bush, was born. Working hard at his studies, George, Sr., completed his college education in economics in only two and a half years. Graduating with top grades, he earned membership in the Phi Beta Kappa honorary fraternity. He was also elected senior class president and was "tapped" (chosen) as a member of Yale's secret society—Skull and Bones.

Rather than accept secure employment in his father's firm, Bush's friend convinced him to go to the Texas oil fields. Starting at an entry-level position as an equipment clerk, Bush learned every aspect of the oil business, working his way up to salesman. By then, George and Barbara had had their second child, Robin.

In the early 1950s, the oil industry was booming, and Bush became very successful and prosperous. Just as their future looked limitless, tragedy struck. After six months of battling leukemia, their four-year-old daughter, Robin, died. After this tragic loss, the Bushes went on to have four other children: future Florida Governor John Ellis "Jeb," Neil, Marvin and Dorothy.

In 1952, Prescott Bush was elected as a Republican senator from Connecticut and served for ten years. George decided to follow his father's example and enter public service. In 1963, he became the chairman of Harris County's Republican Committee. His first bid for the senate was unsuccessful, but he had been "bitten by the bug" and chose to run for Congress in 1966. Republican George Bush defeated his opponent in a primarily Democratic district.

After his re-election to Congress in 1968, Bush was considered a bright star in the Republican Party. In 1970, President Richard Nixon took note of Bush's work in Congress and urged him to run for the Senate again. However, Bush lost his second run for the Senate against conservative-Democrat Lloyd Benson. As a reward for his strong Republican showing in Texas, Nixon appointed Bush as U. S. ambassador to the United Nations.

When President Nixon was re-elected in 1972, he approached Bush to be the chairman of the Republican National Committee. In 1973, Vice-President Spiro Agnew resigned after a bribery scandal. Then, an even greater scandal surfaced. A Senate investigation confirmed that Nixon had ordered a break-in at the Watergate Hotel and the offices of Dr. Daniel Ellsworth to destroy documents regarding the Vietnam War, which would embarrass the administration. Bush found himself trying to bolster sagging morale over the mess in Washington. "It wasn't pleasant in those days to be a party spokesman," one Republican co-worker remembered, "but Bush did it with class and earned a lot of respect in the process." On August 9, 1974, Nixon resigned his position as president of the United States instead of facing impeachment hearings.

The new president, Gerald Ford, recognized Bush's efforts to hold the Republican Party together during this time. As a result, Bush was offered a diplomatic post in France or Great

Britain. Instead, Bush requested to be assigned to the U. S. Liaison Office in China.

In December 1975, President Ford summoned Bush back to the U. S. to help with another fall-out from the Watergate scandal—the reputation of the Central Intelligence Agency (CIA). Ford felt that Bush had the qualities needed to redeem the CIA's tarnished image and to provide new guidelines for the agency. In less than one year, CIA Director Bush appeared before Congress 51 times with straightforward testimony that eased public fears about many CIA secret activities.

In 1977, Bush began his own campaign for the Republican presidential nomination. His strongest opponent was Governor Ronald Reagan of California, who won the candidacy on the first ballot. Bush sat in his hotel room with his family when the phone call came from Reagan, asking him to serve as his vice-presidential candidate.

In the election of 1980, Republican candidates Reagan and Bush won over Democrats Jimmy Carter and Walter Mondale by a huge margin. While the vice presidency is often perceived as a relatively unimportant position, Bush worked hard to play a vital role in the administration. Unfortunately, his first chance at serving as president was when Reagan underwent surgery after an assassination attempt.

In 1984, the incumbent Republican president and vice president ran against Walter Mondale and Geraldine Ferraro and won by a wide margin yet again. In July 1985, Bush again resumed temporary presidential authority when Reagan was operated on for colon cancer.

The Republican National Convention of 1988 unanimously chose George Bush as their candidate for the presidency. Bush ran on a platform of "No New Taxes," promising a "kinder, gentler nation" and a "thousand points of light," which advocated volunteerism. On November 8, 1988, 64-year-old George H. W. Bush was elected as the 41st president of the U. S. It had been 152 years since a vice president went on to be elected president.

When son George W. Bush was elected president in 2000, the Bushes became the first father and son to both be elected president since John Adams (1797) and John Quincy Adams (1825). Within the Bush clan, the first President Bush was referred to as "41" and the second as "43."

Unable to stem a faltering economy and high deficit spending, Bush had to break his promise of no new taxes and, subsequently, lost his bid for re-election to Democrat Bill Clinton.

Later, when asked what the most important things to him were, Bush responded, "my wife and my children." He was once quoted as saying, "I couldn't live without her (Barbara) and she couldn't live without me." The Bushes now enjoy more leisure time in their lives, enjoying their family of four sons, one daughter, their children's spouses and a multitude of grandchildren.

William Clinton

Studies of the early life of President Bill Clinton tell a great deal about who he was as a man and a politician. Biographers often mention that those who had the most impact in his life, for better or worse, were women.

Bill Clinton was born William Jefferson Blythe IV on August 19, 1946, in the small town of Hope, AR. He was named after his father, William Blythe III, who had been killed in a car crash just three months before he was born. His mother, Virginia Cassidy Blythe, was faced with the reality of supporting herself and her son. To complete her nursing training, she took young Bill to stay with her parents in New Orleans for the next two years. Clinton's grandparents (especially his grandmother, Edith Cassidy) were strict disciplinarians who instilled in him the importance of education and racial tolerance, welcoming blacks in their grocery store. They tutored little Bill, then nicknamed "Bubba," teaching him to count and read children's books by the age of three. As an adult, Clinton attributed much of his love of learning and value systems to his grandmother. Sadly, Bill's mother and grandmother had violent arguments, and young Bill often took on the role of mediator. Loving both of them, this was very difficult for him, but he assumed the role of peacekeeper in the family.

Upon returning to Arkansas in 1950, Bubba and Virginia (now a licensed nurse anesthetist) started a new life. Later that same year, Virginia married automobile salesman, Roger Clinton. Two years later, the family moved from Hope to Hot Springs, AR. Virginia and Roger had a son, Roger, Jr., in 1956. In the second grade at St. John's Catholic school, Bill excelled, except for getting a D in conduct for repeatedly shouting out answers without giving others a chance to answer.

Although there wasn't a strong religious influence in his family, Clinton became a devoted Baptist from a very young age. His love of church music prompted him to learn to play the saxophone. On Sunday mornings, he would get up on his own, put on his best clothes and walk the half mile to Park Place Baptist Church to attend services alone. His mother spent her Sundays at the racetrack and was a regular at the Oaklawn racetrack in Hot Springs. She was such a devoted fan of Elvis Presley that Clinton called her out of an operating room to break the news of the singer's sudden death in 1977.

Artist Concept:

"After listening to Clinton's speaking during Hillary's campaign in Aberdeen, SD, we were taken by his charismatic speaking abilities. He has a great ability to connect with all sorts of people . . . So the concept of Clinton giving a public speech was a given," explained the artists.

Sculptor: Lee Leuning | Benefactors: Hani Shafai and Susan Campo

Unfortunately, Roger Clinton, Sr., was an abusive alcoholic who took out his anger on Bill's mother and his sons. He even once shot a gun off in the house. At the age of 14 and already standing more than six-feet tall, Bill finally snapped. He stood up to his stepfather and said, "If you want them, you'll have to go through me." The abuse stopped, but the drinking didn't, and Virginia divorced Roger in 1962. Clinton recalled, "That was a dramatic thing. It made me know I could do it if I had to, but it made me more averse to conflict." Three months later, however, Virginia remarried Roger Clinton, despite her son's vehement opposition. At the age of 16, Bill Blythe legally changed his name to Bill Clinton, taking the name of his stepfather, Roger Clinton, when his half-brother, Roger Clinton, Jr., began to attend school.

Bill attended Hot Springs High School where he was an outstanding student and star member of the jazz band. The principal, Johnny Mae Mackey, placed special emphasis on having her students devote themselves to public service. She developed a strong bond with the smart and politically inclined Clinton. In later years, the president would acclaim Ms. Mackey as one of the strongest influences in his life.

In June 1963, Bill was chosen to represent his state in a mock government called American Legion Boys Nation. He was sent to Washington, D. C., with other Boys Nation state representatives and was invited to the White House. Bill was the first in line to shake President John F. Kennedy's hand. It was then he knew he wanted a career in public service.

After high school graduation in 1964, Clinton attended Georgetown University to study international affairs. He specifically chose Georgetown because of its proximity to Washington, D. C. To earn extra money, he worked as a clerk for the Foreign Relations Committee under Senator William Fulbright, who was one of the most outspoken critics of the Vietnam War. Clinton came to share Fulbright's view that the war was both immoral and contrary to America's best interest.

In 1968, after graduation from Georgetown, Clinton won the highly prestigious Rhodes Scholarship (the only president to do so) to study for two years at Oxford University. Shortly after he arrived in England though, Clinton received his draft notice and had to return to Arkansas. He avoided military service by enrolling in an ROTC program at the University of Arkansas. Instead of attending law school, he returned to Oxford. Apparently feeling guilty about his decision to avoid the draft, Clinton resubmitted his name to the draft board but received a high enough lottery number to assure that he would not have to serve in Vietnam.

Instead of completing his Rhodes Scholarship though, Clinton entered Yale Law School, where he met a bright, young woman named Hillary Rodham. She shared his political ambitions, although she was a politically conservative Republican. Two years after graduation, the couple married on October 11, 1975, in a small ceremony at the home Clinton bought for Hillary as a wedding present. Their only child, Chelsea, was born in 1980. The Clintons then moved to Arkansas where Bill began teaching at the University of Arkansas Law School at Fayetteville and immediately thrust himself into the political arena.

In 1974, Clinton ran for the U. S. House of Representatives but lost. However, the election was so close, it marked him as a rising political star of the Arkansas Democratic Party. Two years later, Clinton was elected state attorney general. In 1978, at the age of 32, he became one of the youngest governors in American history. Hampered by his youth and political inexperience, he lost the re-election. Devastated by the loss, Clinton admitted his mistakes and asked voters to give him another chance. He was re-elected in 1982 and went on to serve as governor for nine years, introducing laws to improve education, enacting welfare reform and appointing record numbers of African-Americans and women to government positions. Hillary worked alongside the governor on many of these programs, beginning her role as chief advisor to Clinton.

In 1992, Clinton, 47, entered the race for president. Despite campaign accusations of draft dodging, questionable financial dealings and rumors of infidelity, Clinton easily defeated competitor President George H. W. Bush. His first years in office were widely unsuccessful, but he was able to enact the "Don't Ask, Don't Tell" policy and ratify the North American Free Trade Association. Through a task force led by First Lady Hillary Clinton, he endorsed a massive health care reform act, but the bill failed to move through Congress and became a massive political disaster.

Toward the end of his first term, Clinton worked hard to restore his popularity by signing a law that added 100,000 policemen and instituted harsher punishment for a variety of crimes. He signed a law to increase the minimum wage. In 1996, Clinton handily defeated Republican Bob Dole to secure a second term.

However, Clinton's reputation suffered from scandals in his personal life. His terms in the White House were dominated by rumors of extramarital affairs, including the Monica Lewinsky scandal. The president first denied and then later admitted that he had had sexual relations with the 22-year-old White House intern. Congress appointed independent prosecutor, Kenneth Starr, to investigate the affair, producing an explicit report with salacious details. In 1998, the Republican-dominated House of Representatives impeached Clinton for lying under oath and for obstruction of justice for his actions in the Lewinsky affair, but the Senate acquitted him on all charges. Throughout the scandal, Hillary stood at her husband's side.

In 2000, despite all the criticisms of him personally and politically, Clinton departed the White House with one of the highest approval ratings of any president in history. This was due in large part to the booming economy, for which he took credit.

Now retired, the Clintons remain active on the political scene. Clinton became involved on the global stage, including the Clinton Climate Initiative to combat climate change and the Clinton Foundation Haiti Fund dedicated to rebuilding Haiti after a devastating 2010 earthquake. He also played an active role in Hillary's failed 2008 presidential bid. Recently, he and George W. Bush have been very active in combating HIV/AIDS in third-world countries. On January 3, 2001, Hillary Clinton became a U. S. senator from New York State. At the present time, Hillary serves as secretary of state under President Barack Obama.

George W. Bush

George Walker Bush grew up with a passionate dream. His father, President George H. W. Bush, and grandfather, Prescott Bush, were prominent in the world of politics. His education included the prestigious Phillips Academy in Andover, MA, Yale and Harvard, and he was born to a family of wealth and influence. However, George wanted one career above all others—to become the major league baseball commissioner.

White House

George was born in New Haven, CT, on July 6, 1946, to George H. W. Bush and Barbara Pierce Bush, the first of six children. His father served as the youngest naval pilot in the Pacific theater during World War II, and his mother was the daughter of a wealthy New York magazine publisher. Upon leaving the military, George's father looked to the wide-open spaces far from New England to be part of the oil boom underway in west Texas. George, Sr., took a job as a $375-a-month clerk in an oil-drilling equipment company in Odessa, TX, when "Georgie" was two years old. On December 20, 1949, Pauline Robinson Bush ("Robin") was born.

In Midland, TX, "Big George" teamed with friends to form an oil-exploration outfit and began a family financial empire. A second son, John Ellis Bush ("Jeb") was born in February of 1953. The next month, a tragedy descended on the Bush family. Robin was diagnosed with advanced leukemia, a disease that was nearly always fatal 50 years ago. Sadly, Robin died two months before her fourth birthday, but George had never been informed of how sick his sister really was. As a result, her death was quite a shock.

George took it upon himself to console his parents. It was at this time that his quirky personality emerged. He not only became the family clown, but he became a clown with a gift. After Robin's death, the family tended to avoid mentioning her, but Barbara did not want to relinquish her daughter to an unspoken name. Young George picked up on this. Once, during a Midland football game, George stood on his tiptoes to see the action on the field and he blurted out, "Dad, I wish I was Robin!" George, Sr., asked why he'd said that.

Artist Concept:

The sculptor wanted to depict Bush's natural optimism. He is shown striding forward, perhaps across the White House lawn towards his helicopter, giving a thumbs up to his countrymen. Best known for biting a reporter, his dog, Barney, is with him.

Sculptor: James Michael Maher | Benefactor: Tim Norberg

"I'll bet she can see the game better from up there than we can from down here," he said, pointing toward the heavens.

The passage of time softened the blow of losing a child. Soon the Bush family grew with three more children and a secure financial future. George did grow up as a happy child, but his carefree approach to life did not stem from innocence, but necessity.

George's academic standings throughout his school and college years were mediocre, at best. Carrying a solid C+ average, even in college, George was more preoccupied with pranks and sports than politics or studies. Like his father, George was an avid baseball fan, football quarterback and basketball player. Still, try as he might, he was never able to achieve the athletic prowess of his father. Possibly his greatest athletic achievement was becoming captain of his cheerleading squad at Andover. Once, George got his fellow cheerleaders to dress in drag, complete with stuffed bras and short skirts.

Always the prankster, George was remembered by Sam Houston Principal John Bizilo. "Old George was a class clown. He was a pretty active boy. He wasn't mean or vicious, but he was the leader of his clan." Bizilo will be remembered as the educator who once paddled little George in the fourth grade for what seemed like the harmless prank of painting sideburns on his face to imitate Elvis Presley.

In his college years, George helped tear down the goal posts when Yale beat Princeton on the road in a football game. He was escorted out of town by the Princeton campus police. A friend of George's said, "He's not a guy who would go off by himself, thinking of something. He's more likely to be hiding in a tree waiting to jump down on somebody."

George was a typical college student. He attended classes, drank beer and dated lots of girls. Despite unimpressive grades, George joined the Delta Kappa Epsilon fraternity as a legacy and was "tapped" to be a member of the Skull and Bones Society, an elite "secret" society of promising students who had invited his father years earlier.

Graduating at the height of the Vietnam War, Bush joined the Texas Air National Guard and was assigned to the 147th Fighter-Interceptor Group, training on F-102 fighters full time. In his last two years with the national guard, he took leave to work on his father's political campaign and then moved to Boston to attend Harvard Business School. Bush was grounded for lack of training hours over those last two years but was honorably discharged on October 1, 1973. This perceived shirking of his military responsibilities became an issue for Democrats during the general presidential election of 2000.

During his Harvard years, 27-year-old George knew exactly where his future would take him. Unlike his fellow MBA candidates who were headed for Wall Street, George planned to return to Texas. Classmates remember George as a character that drove a messy Oldsmobile Cutlass, listened to jazz and sat in the back of the classroom in his bomber jacket chewing tobacco.

In 1977, two events changed George's future. After Harvard, Bush sought to make his fortune in the oil business. Unfortunately, he entered the field at the time that oil drilling was on the downturn. After merging his company with a larger oil and gas company, Bush

made money while others in the industry went broke. His talents were not in discovering new oil and gas wells but in finding investors. By the mid-1980s, Bush left the oil business but not before selling his stock in the company for nearly $850,000.

His second stroke of luck was meeting an attractive school librarian named Laura Welch. Although they met formally at a backyard barbecue in Midland, TX, in 1977, they had attended junior high school at the same time, lived in the same Houston apartment in their 20s and had many mutual friends. Ironically, neither of them remembered the other. Three months later, on November 5, 1977, George and Laura were married and later had twin daughters named Barbara and Jenna. George's marriage to Laura was a turning point in his life. He gave up his partying ways and settled down.

Late in 1988, the Texas Rangers Major League Baseball team was for sale. For Bush, this was his dream come true. It allowed him to combine his love of baseball and his talent for raising money. He joined with a group of investors who made George the front man. George put up $600,000 of his own money to purchase the less-than-stellar team and then built a state-of-the-art ballpark with tax revenues, which made the enterprise financially successful. When Bush finally cashed out of the baseball business to enter politics, he left with an extraordinary profit of $15 million.

In 1992, George ran for governor of Texas and defeated incumbent Ann Richards in 1994. He was re-elected in 1998 in a landslide victory of 1.4 million votes over his opponent. Bush emerged overnight as the man to beat in the upcoming presidential election.

When Bush entered the race against 12 other candidates for the 2000 Republican presidential nomination, he quickly out-maneuvered and out-spent all of them until he became the party's nominee. He ran against Senator Al Gore in one of the most controversial elections in presidential history, based on contested votes in the state of Florida. Because of challenged votes in that state, it took the Supreme Court of Florida until December 9 to declare Bush the winner. Bush won the presidency with only one electoral vote to spare.

During his two-term presidency, the public had a love-hate relationship with him. Often depicted as a political lightweight with an odd vocabulary and an earlier life of questionable behavior, Bush's leadership skills were tested like no other president before him on September 11, 2001. On that day, terrorists hijacked U. S. jetliners, crashing into the World Trade Center buildings in New York City and the Pentagon outside Washington, D. C., killing thousands. This prompted Bush to announce a "War on Terrorism." Bush rallied the nation around the American flag, and his approval rating for handling this national tragedy soared.

After retiring from the presidency in 2009, George and Laura retired to Prairie Chapel, which is their beloved 1500-acre ranch in Crawford, TX, and remain a devoted couple.

2009–
Forty-fourth President of the United States of America

Barack Obama

Barack Obama is the first African American elected to the presidency. Born on August 4, 1961, in Honolulu, HI, he was named after his father, who grew up in a small village in Kenya. When Obama was two years of age, his father returned to Kenya, and young Barack only saw his father once more at the age of ten.

After his mother remarried, she and Barack moved to Jakarta, Indonesia, to live with his stepfather and half-sister. At the age of ten, Obama went back to live with his grandparents in Honolulu.

Obama attended Occidental College in Los Angeles and then transferred to Columbia University in New York. He then entered Harvard Law School, receiving his J. D. degree in 1991, graduating magna cum laude.

And so the story began . . .

This book is written as an expanded tribute to The City of Presidents, located in Rapid City, SD.
From the beginning, it is the policy of the organization to memorialize former United States presidents
and not include seated presidents until they leave office. Therefore, as of the printing of this book,
President Obama is a seated president with a political history yet to be written.
The second printing of this book will include our 44th president along with a photo of his bronze statue.